# SURF CITY
# DRAG CITY

ROB BURT

First published in the UK 1986 by Blandford Press
Link House, West Street, Poole, Dorset BH15 1LL



Distributed in the United States by
Sterling Publishing Co, Inc,
2 Park Avenue, New York, NY 10016

Distributed in Australia by
Capricorn Link (Australia) Pty Ltd
PO Box 665, Lane Cove, NSW 2066

**British Library Cataloguing in Publication Data**

Burt, Rob
Surf city, drag city.
1. Music, Popular (Songs, etc.)—
California—History and criticism
I. Title
780'.42' 09794 ML3477.7.C3

ISBN 0-7137-1890-0
ISBN 0-7137-1891-9 Pbk



Designed and produced by **Rob Burt**

Typeset by Quadraset Ltd, Midsomer Norton, Avon

Printed in Great Britain by
Butler & Tanner Ltd, Frome and London

# SURF CITY
## DRAG CITY

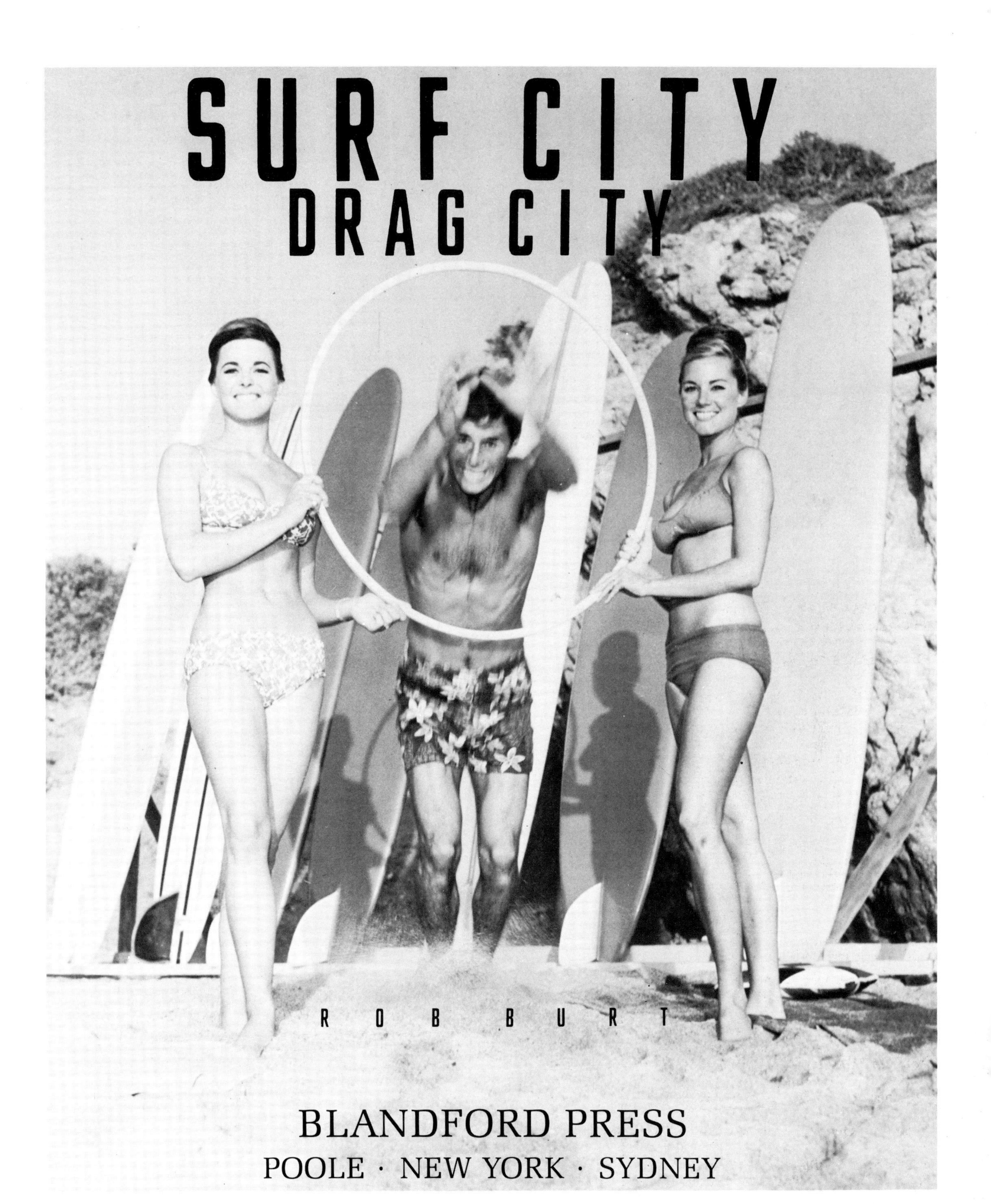

ROB BURT

BLANDFORD PRESS
POOLE · NEW YORK · SYDNEY

# Contents:

THE SURFARIS
FUN CITY,
APACHE
MOON DAWG
SHAZAM
MURPHY THE SURFIE
GO GO GO FOR LOUIE'S PLACE
...and others

STEREO
Vista
STER-3327
ANNETTE Sings
GOLDEN SURFIN' HITS
SIDEWALK SURFIN'
SURFER'S STOMP
SURFIN' U.S.A.
SURFER BOY
SURF CITY
SURFIN' SAFARI
RIDE THE WILD SURF
BALBOA BLUE
BOY TO LOVE
JUST STRICTLY SURFIN'
NO ONE COULD BE PROUDER
Annette
and just for fun
"THE MONKEY'S UNCLE"

CAPITOL FULL DIMENSIONAL STEREO
SCHOOL IS A DRAG
THE SUPER STOCKS FEATURING GARY USHER
SATURDAY'S HERO • LITTLE HONDA • A GUY WITHOUT WHEELS • SCHOOL IS A DRAG • GRIDIRON GOODIE
READIN', RIDIN' AND RACING • LET FREEDOM RING • CLASS DAY • HOT ROD HIGH • SCHOOL BUS BLUES

SURFER GIRL
THE BEACH BOYS
LITTLE DEUCE COUPE • SURFER GIRL • CATCH A WAVE • THE SURFER MOON • SOUTH BAY SURFER • HAWAII
IN MY ROOM • THE ROCKING SURFER • SURFERS RULE • OUR CAR CLUB • YOUR SUMMER DREAM • BOOGIE WOODIE

# The Endless Summer: *Influence & Affluence*

*If everybody had an ocean across the U.S.A.*
*Then everybody be surfin' like Californ-i-a*

*Surfin' U.S.A.* — Brian Wilson

**Southern California in the early sixties had a gracious lifestyle . . . The Golden State that, in its own zany way, caught the youthful spirit and optimism of Kennedy's New Frontier.**

**At its heart lay the sprawling city of Los Angeles — the entertainment capital of the world, famous for its Hollywood movie colony, Disneyland, freeways and summer resort weather twelve months of the year.**

The young Californians' life was one of affluence and fun, cruisin' for chicks, root beer, drive-ins, burgers and beach parties were their staple diet . . . while their preoccupation with the sun-soaked sports of surfing and drag racing provided them with a ready-made image and lifestyle unique to their time and place.

'What are cars and surfboards?' wrote Donald Lyons. 'They are primary colors of American motion. Cars are an active exploitation of natural energy through the machine and surfboards a passive enjoyment of natural energy through bodily skills — two brilliantly characteristic modes of American response to life.'

Looking at the background behind these seemingly opposite phenomenons you begin to discover a certain freewheeling parallel.

Surfing, the recognized sport of Hawaiian kings, was first introduced to California in 1907 by Celtic-Hawaiian surfing pioneer George Freeth. George had been invited by the Pacific Electric Railroad to demonstrate surf-riding at Redondo Beach as a crowd-pulling exercise in an attempt to attract fare paying passengers at weekends.

Although a tough and restricted sport, due mainly to the enormous and heavy redwood boards, it quietly persisted as a minority pursuit along the West Coast until its second great wave of interest during the twenties.

This second wave was heralded by the arrival in California of the Hawaiian Olympic swimming champion Duke Kahanamoku. Duke surfed the California coastline from Malibu to San Onefre, attracting a growing following along the way.

He soon began to coach surfing to many of the Hollywood stars — in much the same way as Bruce Lee was to do for the art of Kung-Fu decades later, and like Lee he also ended up in the movies. His films included *The Wake of The Red Witch* (1948) opposite the Hollywood Duke, John Wayne, and John Ford's *Mr. Roberts* (1955).

Just at the time when the Duke was on the set with the King of the Cowboys, surfing received its biggest shot-in-the-arm; it came

**Above: The late surfing pioneer Duke Kahanamoku.**

**Right: An early little surfer girl.**

via Bob Simmons, a young Californian, and his innovative balsawood and fibre-glass surfboard — better known as the 'Malibu board'.

Simmons became to the beach community the archetypal surfer; a graduate of the Californian Institute of Technology, he spurned a conventional career in favour of the life of a surfbum. He spent his days on the beach building surfboards, surfing or travelling the coast in his beat-up auto in search of the perfect wave.

He also studied charts and maps of the world and predicted some of today's most popular surfing spots — from Mexico to South Africa.

Sadly, Simmons drowned in the surf at Windansea Beach, La Jolla, Calif, before ever proving his theories. Apart from his revolutionary lightweight surfboard Bob is best remembered for projecting the surfer's image as a romatic 'beat' character.

Just as the surfing world was receiving its biggest boost the California hot-rodders were getting their show on the road. The Southern Californian Timing Association had been founded by Art Tilton well before World War II. Unfortunately, Art didn't come home after the war, so it was left to a young hot-rodder by the name of Wally Parks to organize their events.

Prior to the war, the SCTA had held dry lake race meetings at El Mirage, but due to the population explosion in California's southland and their new found post-war auto technology it made the idea of racing on such a short lake-bed an impossibility. So Parks looked further afield, eventually finding the perfect location at Utah's

Bonneville Salt Flats. So by the end of 1948 the SCTA gained permission to hold the first Bonneville Speed Week.

Coinciding with Parks' search for a new raceway, Bob Petersen and Bob Lindsay, two young hot-rod enthusiasts, felt the climate was right to start a publication aimed at their new found passion. Bob Peterson: 'I built cars and played around with them. Nothing too spectacular. Bob Lindsay and I had done a lot of things around hot rods. Lindsay's father had a magazine, and between us — with his father's help — we started on the first issue of *Hot Rod*. We'd seen what was happening and thought it would be a good idea for a magazine.'

The first issue of *Hot Rod* magazine hit the streets in 1947; the following year, riding on the success of the magazine, Peterson formed the Hollywood Associates and staged a custom car show at the Armory at Exposition Park. The show was a huge success, especially for a young customizer by the name of George Barris — whose ultra-wild-looking remodelled Buick stole the show.

Barris had moved to Los Angeles from the State capital Sacramento during the mid-forties and enrolled at the city's Art Center School — a faculty famous for its auto-design course.

As he pulled into the parkin' lot on the first day of term in his customized '36 Ford Coupe he caused a minor sensation for nobody had seen anything quite like it — for his creation sported: push button doors, frenched headlights and an alligator hood. Before even entering his first class he picked-up a number of custom jobs on the strength of his car.

Like so many other LA teenagers, when school was out he'd cruise the streets or hang-out with other hot rodders at one of the many drive-ins — the Piccadilly on the corner of Washington Place and Sepvulveda Boulevard was one of his favourite haunts.

'We'd all be at the Piccadilly or some place, and guys would start challenging each other,' he told Tom Wolfe for *Esquire* magazine. 'You know, a guy goes up to another guy's car and looks up and down like it has gangrene or something, and he

**Left: Early drag racing without the luxury of a custom-built strip.**

**Above: The lobby card says it all.**

**Right: Standing by the ocean raw, Troy and Sandra from *A Summer Place* (1959).**

says: "You wanna go?" "You wanna go for pink slips?" The registration on the cars were pink; in other words, the winner got the other guy's car.

'Well, as soon as a few guys had challenged each other, everybody would ride out onto this stretch of Sepvulveda Boulevard or the old divided highway, in Compton, and the guys would start dragging, one car on one side of the center line, the other car on the other. Go a quarter of a mile. It was wild. Some night there'd be a thousand kids lining the road to watch, boys and girls all sitting on the sides of their cars with the lights shining across the highway.'

Illegal street racing became the 'in' thing around the Los Angeles area; apart from Sepvulveda Blvd other popular venues included Culver Blvd, Rivergrade Road, Avalon Blvd and East 17th Street in Long Beach — that was until the Los Angeles Police Department brought down the heavy hand of the law.

During the next few years several attempts were made to introduce organized drag strips with the idea of keeping the delinquent drag racers off the street.

The first official and commercially run drag strip opened at the Orange County Airport near Santa Ana on July 2, 1950 — many more were to follow during the next decade.

However, the illegal street race never fully disappeared, especially as far as the low-budget movie industry was concerned.

To the sounds of rock 'n' roll they came scorching off the backlot — *Hot Rod Girl* (1956), *Dragstrip Girl* (1957), *Hot Rod Gang* (1958), *Dragstrip Riot* (1958) and *Teenage*

*Thunder* (1959) — all sharing a common theme of hot rodders being nothing more than juvenille delinquents on wheels.

*Hot Rod Girl* is a good example of the genre; the plot follows the attempts by a fair-cop (Chuck Conners) to organize official speed trials and clear his patch of outlawed street racing.

The plot could well have been based on the true story of Officer Bud Coons of the Pomona Police Dept who, with the assistance of his chief, secured permission for a couple of local car clubs to use a runway at the old Fontana Airport for supervised drag racing.

Coons later joined the National Hot Rod Association (a body formed in 1952) as National Field Director and has been credited as the main organizer behind the '53 NHRA Safety Safari — a further attempt to keep blood in the blood-bank and not on the highway . . . 'Ten, four'.

A couple of the hot rod movies even sported real-life drivers — Tommy Ivo, for example, appeared in Edward L Cahn's *Dragstrip Girl* co-starring Fay Spain and Steve Terrell.

Ivo was a popular figure on the drag circuit and among the many highlights of his distinguished career, he was to set top time for a gas dragster in the 1960 Second Annual Bakersfield meet. He clocked 170 mph with an estimated time of 8.97.

A true showman, he also launched the first coast-to-coast performance tour and after its success the competition trail was opened-up for hundreds of other full-time touring pro-drag racers.

Around the end of the fifties Hollywood began looking for other teenage themes to exploit . . . Universal Pictures soon purchased the movie rights to *Gidget*, a novel by Frederick Kohner based on the bohemian lifestyle of his daughter Cathy and her surfing adventures.

The movie, directed by Paul Wendkos, starred the pubescent teen favourite Sandra Dee in the title role while the leading surfmen included the dependable Cliff Robertson and the Philadelphia pop idol James Darren. Darren also recorded the title song.

No sooner had Sandy dried her hair and changed out of her swimsuit she was back in the salty air and on the beach again for

Warner's soppy soaper *A Summer Place* (1959).

An exacting role for the former Alexandra Gluck for not only did she have to contend with the rolling surf but the advances of droppy-eyed Troy Donohue.

Donohue, or Merle Johnson's role, called on him to be a heavy petting beefy in bathers and after the final take he was wearing his heart on his neatly pressed sleeve and telling *Popular Screen*, 'And to think I once regarded her as just a kid! We date a lot these days and she is always great fun — She has made me believe that I can do anything I want to. As a person, she has a sensitivity and a kindness that are really touching — and you can make of that what you want.' Poor boy Troy, for Miss Dee was soon to become Mrs Bobby Darin.

*A Summer Place* is probably best remembered for Max Steiner's lush title theme while *Gidget* (1959) could be described as the first encounter between surf culture and pop music. Albeit a brief cameo by The Four Preps whose *Twenty Five Miles to Catalina* had sailed into the top ten the previous year.

Cliff Robertson's interest in surfing was to take him well beyond his *Gidget* role. 'One day,' he recalled, 'production on the picture got held up while we waited for a shipment of boards to come in from Honolulu, and I got thinking why couldn't the West Coast support a surf board industry. Certainly the sport had progressed far beyond the fad phase.

'So, with a partner, I set up a small operation in Venice, California. We drew some blue prints, bought some raw materials and started to turn out ten or twelve boards a month.'

However, The Robertson Surf Board Company wasn't the only one to catch on to the trend; in Venice alone there was Flaherity Surfboards, Gomes Surfboards and Dewey Webber Surfboards.

But without doubt the recognized new wave of surfboard innovators hailed from Dana Point, and Hobie Surfboards and Santa Monica and Sweet's Surfboards.

**Right: Cliff Robertson makes a dash for Venice . . . and the Surfboard industry (Gidget, 1959).**

Hobie Alter is the man most experts agree first started experimenting with foam plastic while Dave and Roger Sweet are credited for producing the first board manufactured as a one-piece, foam constructed, high density mould.

With the production of these new easier to handle boards, surfing erupted into a whole new way of life. Taking over from the older sportsmen, an enthusiastic group of young people bound together by the surf, set themselves apart. The Surfer was not only different in the way he handled his board, but by the way he dressed. He wore pendletons, white levis, baggies; his hair was sun-bleached (or helped a little by peroxide) and he used his own slang vocabulary.

Another important factor was with the introduction of these super lightweight boards, girls took an even greater role in the sport and were soon turning out champions such as Wendy Cameron, Anona Naone and Nancy Nelson.

Left: . . . Hobie Alter, of course.

**Bruce Brown — "A Bergman of the boards".**

The surfing cult also had its own publication; John Severson's *Surfer* magazine based at Dana Point — starting life as a cheapie production it quickly developed into a full-scale full-colour glossy. During the early sixties surf boom publisher Severson lent his name to a Capitol Records surf album.

*John Severson Presents Sunset Surf*, produced by Nick Venet and featuring the music of Jimmie Haskell. Among the programme of tracks it features *Murphy's Grey Wet Suit* — a tribute to the magazine's cartoon hero, illustrated by the up and coming artist Rick Griffin. Griffin would later find fame as the San Francisco scene's leading poster designer.

Severson's surfing interest didn't stop at the magazine, for he was also a member of a small group of bona fide surf movie makers. The group included Phil Wilson, Bruce Brown and Gregg Noll (Noll can be seen dwarfed by a giant wave at Hawaii's famous Pipeline among the opening credits of John Miliu's surf nostalgia movie *Big Wednesday* (1978).

A completely dedicated and authoritative bunch — Brown, for example, started surfing at the age of twelve. Rising at dawn, he would steal two precious hours of surfing at California's Alamitos Bay before heading off to school.

While at high school he became interested in film-making and it wasn't long before he was screening his first surf footage in his parents' garage to the delight of the neighbourhood kids.

After graduating he continued with his twin-passion of surfing and film making and by 1959, at the age of twenty-one, he released his first full-length surf movie *Slippery When Wet*, quickly followed by *Surf Crazy* (1960).

By the time *Barefoot Adventure* (1961) was released he'd picked up quite a following among Californian teenagers. His following increased, however, after *Water Logged* (1962) a compilation of all his best action sequences.

With the success of his latter films, Brown embarked on his most ambitious project . . . *The Endless Summer*.

For *The Endless Summer* Bruce enlisted two young Californian surfers Mike Hynson and Robert August and took them on a surfin' safari around the world.

Among their many discoveries, the trio found the goal of all surfers — the perfect wave.

This they discovered at Cape St. Francis, South Africa, now a surfers' legend, where wave after wave is so perfect as to appear machine made.

In Hawaii he produced his best action footage to date, filming some of the world's best surfers, riding the giant 25 foot waves at Waimea Bay and shooting the curl at the infamous Pipeline.

Bruce used over nine miles of film that he eventually edited down to a mere 8223 feet. When *The Endless Summer* was finally released in 1966 *Life* magazine called it 'The nicest surprise to happen in the low-budget movie business in a long time'. *Newsweek*'s review started 'One of the year's ten best films'. While *Time* magazine added 'A dazzling ode to sun, sand and surf' and even described Bruce Brown as 'A Bergman of the boards'.

It has been the accepted practice for the genre to use a modern jazz soundtrack (perhaps as a throw-back to the sports bohemian origins). *Barefoot Adventure* for example featured saxman Bud Shank and his group while Phil Wilson's *Gone With The Wave* included the sympathetic sounds of Lalo Schifrin.

Among other things *The Endless Summer* changed all that, by featuring the music of The Sandals — a little known surf group from San Clemente, who had previously made a big impression at the First Annual Surfing Fair held at the Long Beach Civic Auditorium.

The impact of the above mentioned movies on West Coast teenagers, coupled with all the latest developments, helped establish an atmosphere that soon took surfing beyond the realms of a sporting activity. Pop graphics and kandy kolors appeared on cars and surfboards alike. And 'Decals' became the 'in thing'. The construction of the Los Angeles freeway network made the beaches and drag strips even more accessible — further influencing their individual popularity.

Schools were divided into surfers and Hodads (a term used to describe hot-rodders) who kept up a tribal rivalry in much the same way as the UK Mods and Rockers.

The hot rod cult had also been progressing happily along its own road; at Bonne-

**The Sandals**

**Above: Burnin' rubber Ed Kookie Byrns from Warner Bros. TV series *77 Sunset Strip*.**

ville, Doc Ostich made his debut in The Flying Caduceus — the first jet car that was to blaze the trail for speed-merchant Craig Breedlove who, in his Spirit of America, became the fastest man on three wheels.

Under a hoarding 'Kustom City' George Barris took-up residence at 10811 Riverside Drive, North Hollywood and boasted among his many clients Elvis Presley, Jayne Mansfield and Liberace.

He had also began supplying his grand-auto's to the film and TV world, his XM: SC-210, for example, became a regular feature on the *Dobie Gillis* TV series. Basically a '31 Ford body, the XM featured a chopped top and slanted windshield and a unique streamlined hood created from a pair of 1940 Ford hoods welded face to face. Under the hood lay a supercharged fuel-injected Oldsmobile that clocked 198 mph at Bonneville.

Warner's *77 Sunset Strip* became undoubtedly the most popular TV series featuring hot rod culture. What caught the public's imagination was the character Gerald Lloyd Kooksan III, better known as Kookie — the hair combing, hot rodding, jive talkin' Dino's Diner parkin' lot attendant who in his hip way became a kind of folk hero of modern mobilized California.

The role of Kookie was played by Ed Byrnes with such conviction that he gained the million selling single *Kookie, Kookie, Lend Me Your Comb* on the strength of it.

Ed was joined on the disc by Connie Stevens of *Sixteen Reasons* fame. Frock 'n' roll queen Connie, also starred in *Sunset Strip*'s TV cousin *Hawaiian Eye* as Cricket opposite the highly underrated Hawaiian actor with the unfortunate name of Poncie Ponce.

Warner Brothers finally milked the TV youth-orientated private-eye genre dry with the suitably fashionable *Surfside Six*. Featuring forever freshman Troy Donohue in the lead.

At the height of his TV popularity Byrnes was asked if off screen did he resemble the character of Kookie in any way? 'Well, I don't talk like him,' he replied. 'But I do admire his free and easy personality, and I guess I'm like him in some ways.'

Top teen-idols Ed Byrnes, Sandra Dee, Troy Donohue and Connie Stevens' on-screen image epitomized the new West Coast youth culture with their love of the beach and fast cars.

The youth of California were united by their affluence, the sunshine, and their addiction to the casual life. Their love of the physical sport of riding a wave was matched, somehow, by an aesthetic if not to say spiritual thrill of being carried by the forces of nature.

Perhaps it is this that joined surfers in a bond more firm that the usual bond between fellow sportsmen. They shared a thrill, and talked about the experience rather than simply the technique. Perhaps it was this spiritual bond that accounted for the difference between this group and others, that brought about a folklore, and a music . . .

Prior to the wake of the surf music craze, there were a number of groups popular with surfers — The Gamblers of *Moon Dawg* fame, The Belairs and Dick Dale's Deltones attracted a beach load of teenagers to their surfside dances. While the Chicano influence of Ritchie Valens appealed to surfers and ho-dads alike.

Del-Fi Records' Bob Keene discovered seventeen year old Ritchie playing with his group The Silhouettes at a gig in LA's San Fernando Valley and soon produced his first big hit *Come On, Let's Go.* 'We stuck to an all-guitar format to complement Ritchie's Latin background,' Keene recalled. *Come On, Let's Go* was cut live and Rene Hall overdubbed a 'Danyelectro' guitar to get that clicky sound, and the Goldstar echo helped some. I used the same line-up on The Addrisi Brothers' *It's Love* and Chan Romero's *Hippy, Hippy Shake.*'

Velens' second hit *La Bamba* coupled with *Donna* became a million seller and had Keene retorting: 'I didn't know it, but they were both A-sides; I should've kept one back.'

Dick Dale, a young rock 'n' roller who had also cut a few discs for Keene, remembered: 'Back in the fifties I thought Eddie Cochran was good. Ritchie Valens was another one that I felt was truly great. As a matter of fact, we had the same manager for a while. I remember at his first major stage appearance in Long Beach with me, he only had two songs prepared to do on stage, *La Bamba* and *Donna*. Well, the audience gave him a standing ovation and wanted him back for more.

'Ritchie was backstage wondering what to do and I told him just go back out there and do *La Bamba* again. He did that song three times and every time I said go back and do it again.'

Sadly Valens died in the fateful plane crash that also robbed the world of Buddy Holly and The Big Bopper. The Valens' legacy carried on via Chan Romero and a young high school graduate from Hawthorne by the name of Chris Montez. Chris made his recording debut in 1960 at the age of seventeen with *She's My Rocking Baby*. During the same year he was introduced to ex-Indigo writer/producer Jim Lee who was in the process of setting up his own label — Monogram Records. For his first outing under Lee's supervision *All You Had To Do Was Tell Me*, a duet with Kathy Young, became a considerable local hit. But its follow-up the infectious *Let's Dance* became almost overnight a million seller. Released in the summer of '62 it was quickly followed by another big hit in the form of *Some Kinda Fun*.

After *Some Kinda Fun*, Chris' chart career went into a steep decline until he was signed to Herb Alpert's A&M label in the mid-sixties. At A&M, Montez made a string of MOR hits, *The More I See You* begs a mention only for its promo film, which featured Chris surfing on to the beach to lip synch to a beauty laying on the sand. Chicano rock also flourished in the late fifties and early sixties via the instrumental outfit The Champs. Formed by Dave Burgess, the line-up featured Jimmy Seals, Dash Crofts, Bobby Morris and Dale Morris. The group signed to Gene Autry's Challenge label in '58 and were named after the cowboy star's famous horse. Their first disc *Tequila* (written by Chuck Rio) became the number one disc in the US for five consecutive weeks and also picked-up a Grammy Award for (of all things) best rhythm and blues recording of 1958.

Other hits followed including *El Rancho Rock*, *Cielito Lindo* and *Too Much Tequila* among others. Dave Burgess: 'In late 1961, I

**Left: Richie Valens, a tragic loss to the LA music scene.**

retired from the group to go to work for Gene Autry full-time and I hired Glen Campbell to become the lead guitar player, vocalist and front man for the Champs.' Campbell was born in Delight, Arkansas in 1936, and by the age of six he had became a competent guitarist. He joined his uncle's western band while still a teenager before moving to New Mexico and forming his own outfit. The group later disbanded and armed with his twelve-string guitar Glen landed in Hollywood seeking session work . . . He never looked back. Apart from his early work with The Champs and The Piltdown Men (who scored with *Brontosaurus Stomp* in Sept '60) he went on to appear on a host of Beach Boys, Jan and Dean and other surf and hot rod discs before eventually becoming a huge recording star in his own right.

**Below: The Teddy Bears — Phil Spector, Annette Bard (later to become known as Carol Conners) and Marshall Lieb.**

But, of all the early pioneers that helped put Los Angeles on the recording map Phil Spector's name and unique talent can't be ignored. Famous for his 'Wall of Sound', Spector became a guiding light for The Beach Boys, The Beatles and many others. Phil was a skinny kid of nine years when his mother brought him to California from his Bronx birthplace, after the death of his father. While attending Fairfax High School he formed a singing group with Annette Bard (Kleinbard) and Marshall Lieb. Calling themselves The Teddy Bears, they booked themselves into a LA studio and cut a demo of *To Know Him Is To Love Him*. This original composition by Phil was inspired by the inscription on his father's gravestone and was soon leased to Dore Records. It quickly rose to number one in the nation on 28/9/58; changing to Imperial Records they scored again with *Oh Why* and *I Don't Need You Anymore* in 1959.

Soon after the group disbanded, Phil split to New York to become an interpreter at the UN. The night before his interview he fell in with some musicians and never got there, instead he wrote *Spanish Harlem* and within a year had formed his own label, Philles Records. As a producer on his own label, he became responsible for a multitude of hits by such groups as The Crystals, The Ronettes, Bob B. Soxx and The Blue Jeans and many others . . . soon earning the title 'The first Tycoon of Teen'. As for the other members of The Teddy Bears: Marshall Lieb formed the LA based Marsh label and Annette changed her name to Carol Connors and co-wrote one of the biggest ever hot rod hits while also contributing songs to Dick Dale among many others. Dick Dale and his group the Deltones; Bill Barber, Rick & Barry Dilleria, Nick O'Malley, Jerry Stevens and Frank Armando were becoming firm favourites with the surfin' crowd down at The Rendezvous Ballroom Balboa, although their music at the time was heavily R&B influenced.

Pete Johnson of The Belairs remembered the era. 'We were living in the South Bay area of Los Angeles — the heart of the beach community — and I hung out at the ocean a lot; I surfed a little — mostly body surfing rather than on a board — but I was so involved with my music that it meant very

little to me whether I was identified as a "surfer". It was natural, though, that when we began to get out and around it would be the local surfers who would make up our audience.'

Johnson formed The Belairs in 1960 with Ed Bertrand and the group featured Richard Delvy on the drums. A year later they had a huge regional smash-hit with *Mr. Moto*. After the group disbanded Delvy went on to form The Challengers.

Johnson again: 'We twice had to graduate to larger halls to accommodate the growing crowds, our last such event of the season was at the Hermosa Biltmore Hotel Ballroom. The only other popular live music venues in the greater LA area were the El Monte Legion Stadium (in East LA and STRICTLY ho-dad) and The Rendezvous Ballroom in Balboa, about 40 miles down the coast. It held well over a 1000 (and was usually packed with surfers) and Dale's sound was, in a word awesome! the music was huge and throbbing, especially when combined with all those sandals stomping on the wooden floor — conflict was almost certain when Ho-dads would risk showing up to hear the band.'

Finding that his audience was mainly made up of surfers, Dale started to experiment with a style he was to call 'the surfing sound'. 'It just came out of me,' he said. 'One day I started picking faster and faster like a locomotive. I wanted it to sound hard and powerful. There wasn't anybody who influenced it actually. I mean, there is nothing to influence you once you create a style and stick to that style.'

Dick Dale's surfin' sound created a wave that American teenagers would ride for the next half-decade.

# Glossary of Surfing Terms

**Above the peak:** Above usually means northerly of the peak, along the line of the swell; left or right of the peak.

**Backwash:** Flow of water off the incline of the beach which rushes back to the ocean after a breaker has washed up onto the shore.

**Baggies:** Extremely large, boxer-style trunks worn by many surfers.

**Bail out:** To jump or dive off the surfboard.

**Barge:** A big cumbersome surfboard.

**Belly board:** A small board used in body surfing to add buoyancy and manoeuvreability to the participant; usually a board that is less than three feet in length; sometimes a skim board.

**Big Gun:** A surfboard designed for riding big waves.

**Blown out:** Non-surfable conditions caused by strong winds.

**Body surfer:** One who rides the waves without a board.

**Bottom turn:** A turn made at the bottom of, or out in front of, a wave.

**Bunny (or honey):** A girl surfer, or a surfer's girlfriend.

**Crack:** Australian term for a ride, '. . . let's crack a few waves, Mate.'

**Curl:** The concave part of a wave just as it is breaking; the face of a breaker as the crest curls forward; the hook; the tunnel; the tube.

**Cut-back:** To turn back into the hook of the wave; to ride toward the hook instead of away from it.

**Ding:** Damage to a surfboard.

**Drop:** The steepest part of the wave; usually referred to in describing a take-off; a condition peculiar to the sudden build-up of the crest of the wave as it hits the backwash; also, characteristic of the take-off situation at certain surfing locations and under certain ocean conditions.

**Dumper:** Crashing or plunging wave.

**Elephant gun:** A big wave board.

**Face of the wave:** Steep concave front of the wave which faces shore.

**Fetch:** The distance over which the wind can catch the water and create swells; length of fetch influences the height of the wave.

**Fun surf:** Small or medium size surf — three to six feet.

**Glassy:** Smooth water surface; not choppy; merely a swell condition.

**Go behind:** To pass another surfer on the seaward side of the wave.

**Goofy foot:** A rider who places his right foot ahead of his left, opposed to the standard stance: left ahead of right foot.

**Green back:** A swell, outside, that has not yet broken.

**Gremlin (or gremmie):** A pseudo-surfer; someone who pretends he surfs or a young mischievous surfer.

**Hairy:** Spooky; difficult to surf; big or extremely fast surf.

**Hang ten:** Ten toes protruding over the nose of the surfboard while riding a wave; also, hang five: toes of one foot over the nose of the board.

**Heavies:** Big surf.

**Head dip:** A hot dogging stunt; dipping the head into the wall.

**Ho-dad:** A greaser — hot rodder or non-surfer.

**Hook:** The part of the wave that curls.

**Hot dog:** To show off or do tricks on the surfboard, like 'hanging ten'.

**Humpers:** Large, unbroken waves.

**Hung up:** Riding on the hook or along a steep wall; unable to pull out of the wave.

**Island, island pull-out:** A nose pull-out; to quit the ride by going to the nose of the board and forcing it under the water.

**Kick, kick out, kick turn:** To step on the rear of the surfboard with considerable force and, at the same time, raise the lead foot, lifting the nose of the board out of the water, making it possible to pivot the board on its tail.

**Kook:** A novice surfer; poorly skilled surfer; a beginner or non-surfer.

**Locked in:** A surfer completely covered by the breaking wave and still riding.

**Log:** A very heavy surfboard.

**Make the wave:** To get across the wall or out of the hook before it breaks upon the rider and board.

**Malibu board:** A lightweight surfboard constructed of balsa-wood with a fibre-glass cover; a small manoeuvreable surfboard; a Simmons board.

**Normal size surfboard:** A surfboard providing just adequate buoyancy neither too large nor to small.

**Open door:** A wave that breaks in such a manner that the surfer can ride away from the peak, out of the hook, onto the shoulder. Open door right or left refers to the direction the surfer must turn in order to reach the shoulder.

**Out of control:** Very large breakers; big surf.

**Outside:** The far side of the breaker, seaward of the swell.

**Paddleboard:** A hollow craft designed for paddling — not a surfboard.

**Pass over:** To pass another surfer on a wave by sliding past high on the wave; a go-behind.

**Pass under:** To pass a surfer on the shoreward side while riding the wave.

**Peak:** The highest point of a particular swell; the first portion of the swell to break; the steepest part of the swell.

**Pearling:** Being thrown off by having the nose of the board go down.

**Pick up a wave:** Catch a wave; get a ride.

**Pipeline:** Apart from the famous Hawaiian location — the curl of a wave, before it breaks.

**Plunging surf:** Crashing surf.

**Poly:** Surfboard made of polyurethane.

**Pop-out:** A cheap surfboard.

**Pumped up:** Very excited as a result of good rides.

**Rails:** Edges of surfboard; the sides.

**Reverse, reverse kick-out:** A fancy kick-out style in which the surfboard and ride turn in opposite directions.

**Reverse take-off, reverse skeg take-off:** A take-off stunt which is executed by catching the wave while the surfboard is in a reversed position — skeg pointing shoreward. As the wave is caught, the board is quickly turned around to assume the normal attitude.

**Rock dance:** Walking over rocks, usually at low tide, to retrieve the surfboard.

**Scratching:** Paddling hard.

**Set:** A train of waves; a series of waves following in succession.

**Shape:** Outline of the surfboard; plan view; silhouette presented when looking directly at the deck or belly of the surfboard.

**Shoot, shoot the wave, Shoot the curl:** Ride a wave; get across a critical situation.

**Showboating:** Hot dogging.

**Shuffle:** Moving the weight forward or backward without crossing the legs; sliding the feel along the deck surface.

**Skeg:** Fin.

**Skim board:** Small rectangular or disk-shaped board, usually plywood, used to skim over the shallow water washed up the beach from the force of the wave; belly board.

**Slow surf:** Surfing conditions which are not conducive to fast rides; swells with a very gentle slope and feathering crest.

**Soup:** Swash: the foaming, swirling water which results from the crest of the breaker falling forward.

**South bay:** Tail of the surfboard squared off at the end.

**Spooky:** A difficult or unpredictable surf condition.

**Spoon:** The upturn of the nose of the surfboard; serves same purpose as the rocker.

**Stall:** To throw the board out of trim so that it is no longer sliding.

**Straight off:** To ride the surfboard directly shoreward, not angling across the wave and out onto the shoulder.

**Stick:** A surfboard.

**Stoked:** Excited.

**Surf bumps:** Common calcium deposits on knees and insteps, from kneeling on a surfboard while paddling.

**Swash:** Soup; foaming water after the wave breaks.

**Taking gas:** Being knocked from surfboard by wave. A bad wipe-out.

**The axe:** When the surfer has a wave break on top of him or otherwise knock him off his board, it is said he 'got the axe'; a wipe-out.

**Trimming the board:** Distributing the weight of the surfboard so that it lies flat against the water surface.

**Trough:** The depression in front of the breaker; the negative oscillation of a wave.

**Tubes:** Very hollow waves.

**Turn-around:** A hot-dog stunt where the surfer turns his position completely around, 360 degrees so that at one point he is riding the board backwards.

**Up:** Descriptive of big surf.

**Wax:** Paraffin; to apply paraffin to the deck of the board.

**Wedge:** A board constructed in such a manner that the stringers are placed diagonally through the board and join at the nose.

**White water:** The foam on a breaking wave.

**Wipe-out:** Falling off or being thrown from a surfboard.

**Woodie:** A wooden sided station wagon surfers use to haul their board.

# Glossary of Drag Racing Terms

**Asphalt eater:** Exceptionally fine performing drag racing car.
**Banzai:** Exceptionally hard run over the quarter-mile as a 'banzai run'.
**Barrel:** Cylinder.
**Bash:** A racing event.
**Bleach:** Liquid household bleach poured under rear wheels for burnout.
**Bleach box:** Area well behind starting line for bleach burnouts.
**Bite:** Traction.
**Blower:** Supercharger.
**Boss:** Great.
**Break:** Damage an engine or some part of car.
**Bubble:** Last position in qualifying lineup.
**Bug catcher:** Air scoop for supercharger.
**Burnout:** Spinning rear wheels quickly in puddles of liquid bleach to heat up and clean off tires for maximum traction.
**Bye run:** Single run without an opponent. NHRA rules require that, in elimination competition, if the number of cars is uneven, the odd number car must still make a run even though it is to be unopposed at that time.



**Cam:** Camshaft.
**Charger:** Top performing driver.
**Christmas tree:** Electronic starting system employing a set of countdown lights for each and including green GO lights.
**Chrondeks:** Brand of timers.
**Cog:** Transmission gear or rear end gear.
**Cuda:** Plymouth Barracuda.
**DOHC:** Double overhead camshaft engine. Also SOHC for single cam.
**Dragster:** Machine designed especially for rapid acceleration.
**Drive around:** Catch up and pass opponent after a late start.
**Drop the hammer:** Release the clutch quickly.
**Digger:** AA/Fuel or AA/Gas dragster.
**Eliminate:** Defeat an opponent in a drag race.
**E.T.:** Elapsed time.
**Elephant:** 426 cu in Hemi Dodge or Plymouth engine.
**Eyeball:** Inspect or examine something.
**Funny car:** Specific class of drag racing vehicle made up of a dragster chassis and fitted with plastic body replica of modern passenger car.
**Fuel:** Nitromethane used to increase power and performance.
**Fueler:** Car utilizing exotic fuel.
**Gas couple or sedan:** Specific class of cars which run on stock gasoline. Extensive engine modifications and/or swaps are permitted, but car must retain legal street equipment such as headlight and fenders.
**Handicap:** Head start given slower vehicle when two cars of different classes are racing together.
**Hang it out:** Gamble on a red light start and foul by accelerating off the starting line just before the green light flashes.
**Hang out the laundry:** Deploy parachute brake.
**Hauler:** Hard running driver or car.
**Headers:** Exhaust pipes, designed for free flow.
**Hemi:** Short for Chrysler's engine equipped with hemispherical combustion chambers.
**History:** Destroyed or defeated, such as 'you are now history'.
**Hole shot:** Getting the jump on an opponent at starting line.
**Honk:** Run fast.
**Hot shoe:** Top ranking driver.
**Huffer:** Supercharger.
**Injected:** Engine equipped with fuel injection rather than carburettor.
**Joe log bolt:** Competitor who runs only on weekends, periodically.
**Jug:** Carburettor.
**Juice:** Special exotic fuel.
**Lights:** Timing lights at starting line and at end of quarter-mile.
**Lose fire:** Stall the engine.
**Loud pedal:** Accelerator or throttle.
**Lunch:** Damager engine or other parts severely.
**Mayflower:** Plymouth.
**Mopar:** Chrysler product.
**Motor mouth:** Loud mouth.
**Nerd:** Not hep.
**Nitro:** Short for nitromethane, a fuel additive.
**Off the line:** Leaving the starting line.
**Out to lunch:** Not with it.
**Overstage:** Move the front wheels too far foward at the starting line.
**Puffer:** Supercharger.
**Put it to the wood:** Apply full throttle.
**Rail:** Dragster with long frame rails, sometimes called slingshot.
**Ratchet jaw:** Person who talks too much.

**Rat motor:** 427-cubic-inch Chevy engine.

**Scatter shield:** Protective steel housing around clutch and fly-wheel assembly.

**Short block:** An engine block without heads, manifolds.

**Shut down:** Beat an opponent.

**Shut off:** Slow down before completing run.

**Slicks:** Special tires designed for maximum traction.

**Slush pump:** Automatic transmission.

**Solo:** Single run.

**Stage:** Line up properly at the starting line.

**Staging area:** Area between pits and starting line where cars are assembled by class or category just prior to racing.

**Street machine:** Car suitable for highway driving as well as racing.

**Street race:** Illegal race on public roads, frowned on by legitimate drag racers.

**Terminal Speed:** MPH registered at end of quarter-mile. This is measured electronically from a 166-foot trap at either end of the quarter-mile finish line.

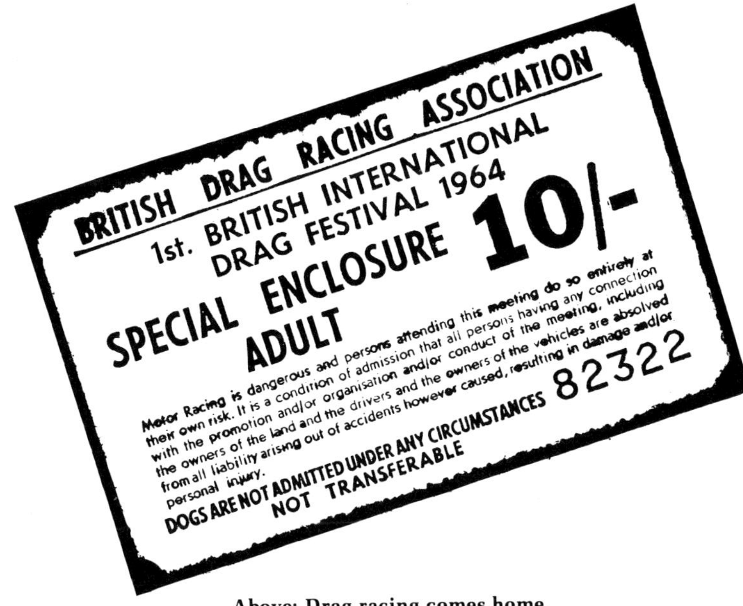


**Above: Drag racing comes home.**

**Tip the can:** Increase percentage of nitromethane.

**Vette:** Corvette.

KFWB #1
KRLA #1
MUSIC CITY
HIT LIST
#1. PEPPERMINT MAN
#5020
#2. MISIRLOU
#5019
#2. SURFER'S CHOICE
L.P. #1001
DEL-TONE
K/MEN #1
KAFY #2
DICK
"SURFER'S
CHOICE"
#1001
The HOTTEST LP in L.A.
SOLD OVER 50,000!
PL. 6-7844

# Surfbeat: *Dick Dale & The Instrumental Swell*

*From Balboa to Anaheim, San Bernadino to Riverside*
*All the kids in old L.A. love to hear Dick Dale play*

*The King of the Surf Guitar* — Alphonso B. Willis

**Beach Boy Mike Love was once asked to define the surfing sound, he replied simply, 'It's just beat music with surfing words.' These are not words Dick Dale, the recognized inventor of surf music and the man it has been said melted plastic guitar picks in a single song, would agree with. He had this to say on the subject: 'Real surfing music is instrumental . . . characterized by heavy staccato picking on a Fender Stratocaster guitar, and it has to be a Stratocaster.'**

Born in Beruit, Dale (real name Monsour) grew up on the Californian beaches as one of the Surfing Community. But from the first he set himself apart from the usual sun-bleached beach image and instead took on an almost gypsy like appearance complete with pierced ear and single gold earring.

This innate individualism was reflected in his music which was to be different from the then recognized West Coast sound. His mastery of a variety of instruments from the guitar to the trumpet and, more importantly perhaps, his electronics expertise, enabled him to become an innovator. Dale's interest in the world of speakers, woofers and tweeters led him to work very closely with Leo Fender (President of Fender Instruments) and together they improved the famous Showman amplifier and developed the reverb unit that gave instrumental surf music its highly distinctive sound.

Outside the workshop and dance hall, Dick lived on the beach and surfed daily. During the summer of '61 he started experimenting with the music he was to call 'The Surfing Sound', which grew out of his desire to create music that somehow matched the feeling he had while hot-doggin' on his surfboard. 'There was a tremendous amount of power I felt while surfing,' he said, 'and that feeling of power was simply transferred from myself into my guitar when I was playing surf music. I couldn't get that feeling by singing, so the music took an instrumental form.'

Dick and his group The Deltones had been playing weekend dances at The Rendezvous Ballroom, Balboa and word

And it has to be a Stratocaster?

spread quickly. In a very short time he was attracting huge crowds — and had earned himself the title 'The Pied Piper of Balboa'.

West Coast DJ and record producer Jim Pewter remembered the period well: 'When I first hit the West Coast during 1961 the word was "Let's go to a Dick Dale dance", so my girl and I motivated to the Rendezvous and checked it out, only to return again and again.'

Dick also recalled this early success. 'We started at the Rendezvous in Balboa, which was way down on the end of the peninsula, and they said nobody would come to my dances because the Ballroom was too far away and nobody will want to drive that distance. We played there for nearly three years and had about 4,000 kids every night we were there.'

**Dick Dale: King of the Surf Guitar.**

Dale and his doting father-manager James Monsour formed The Deltone record label and in September '61 released the group's debut single, the raunchious *Let's Go Trippin'*. The disc soon topped the California charts and even found a placing in the national hot hundred. After *Trippin'* his local popularity increased so much that the authorities threatened to close down The Rendezvous because of the traffic hazard it created — it was not unusual for a line of parked cars to stretch from Newport Beach to the Coast Highway.

November '62 saw the release of his first album, *Surfer's Choice*. Produced by James Monsour, the album was recorded live at a Harmony Park performance, and besides *Let's Go Trippin'* it included many of his most popular on-stage instrumentals including *Surfbeat*, *Surfing Drums* and *Shake 'N' Stomp*.

*Shake 'N' Stomp* had previously been released as the B-side of The Deltones second single *Jungle Fever*, and has a story all of its own. Dale had noticed the kids at his dances were always doing a particular type of dance step . . . when he asked a group of them what it was, they answered 'The Surfer's Stomp'. So Dick recorded the tune and started billing himself as 'The King of the Stomp'.

However, Dale's stomp was beaten to the national charts by The Marketts' *Surfer's Stomp* which reached number thirty-one in the country.

The Marketts were reported to have been a five man outfit hailing from Balboa, but most experts agree that they were in fact session musicians brought together by producer Joe Saraceno who also composed the song, after attending a Dick Dale concert at The Rendczvous.

Saraceno took The Marketts up the charts again with *Balboa Blue*, a tune that owed more to the Bert Kaempfert school of arranging than the feeling you get while riding the waves.

Saraceno was also involved with The Routers who gained a top twenty hit in the same year with *Let's Go*.

The Routers included Mick Gordon, Rene Hall, Sid Sharp, Ed Kay and for a short time Scott Engel who, with John Maus, recorded

**Above: The Routers.**

*Moongoon Stomp* as The Moongooners in '62 before setting sail for England and fame as two-thirds of the Walker Brothers.

Dick Dale may have experienced a setback by being topped by *Surfer's Stomp*, but his third single *Miserlou* became the all-time classic surf instrumental, and would eventually be covered by everyone from The Beach Boys to The Surfaris. *Miserlou* was in fact based on an ancient Greek melody, but who would have believed it, listening to Dick Dale's rendition. His fast and heavy guitar licks were perfectly enhanced by a Mariachi-inspired trumpet solo (also played by Dale), that injected *Miserlou* with a very definite contemporary Californian feel.

Dale had to all intents and purposes captured on record the spirit of California's past and present in one take — it rocketed to the top of Radio KFWB's Fabulous Forty Survey. Suddenly, the sound that Dick Dale and The Deltones had pioneered exploded into a national fad, with many of the local high school garage bands that followed in his wake achieving greater chart action than Dale himself.

Dick was not oblivious to his growing influence: 'There was actually very little happening during the first two years I started playing surf music. After about two and a half years, surf bands started to spring up. I remember The Surfaris and The Pyramids and it was about this time that I started to actually meet certain people at my dances like Jan and Dean, The Beach Boys and Jimi Hendrix, who said that he patterned his guitar style after me.'

Hendrix also said, 'May we never hear surf music again.' — An opinion certainly not shared by the twenty-one thousand fans who turned up for Dick's '61 Los Angeles Sports Arena Concert and sent his records to the top of the Californian charts.

With so much popularity in Southern

**Above: Dick Dale at the beach.**

**Far right: Typical Hilder Del-Fi product.**

California it wasn't long before Dale was picked-up by one of the major record companies. That honour fell to Capitol Records, already the home of The Beach Boys and many lesser known surf groups.

Voyle Gilmore signed Dick to the label in February '63 and took a personal interest in his career. He began by co-producing Dale's first Capitol album *King Of The Surf Guitar* and organizing a massive publicity campaign.

Prior to its release in June '63 Capitol reissued two Deltone singles, *Miserlou* and *Peppermint Man*, and the '62 *Surfer's Choice* album. The releases coincided with a hail of publicity that read . . . 'The Phenomenal DICK DALE teen America's New Favourite. . . . On November 1, 1962 *Surfer's Choice* was released. The album has sold seventy-five thousand in Southern California alone in three months! This is the story of this skyrocketing new star.' It went on to compare the Dick Dale phenomenon with that of Sinatra and Presley before climaxing with 'Dick Dale is something new, entirely different. His style is unique.'

The start of '63 looked very promising for Dick. Not only had he landed the Capitol deal but also his first movie appearance in William Asher's *Beach Party*.

During the summer he toured the US promoting the movie in a string of one-night stands, but unfortunately the hits weren't forthcoming. His biggest national chart breaker, *The Scavenger*, only managed to limp into the hot hundred in the October. *The Scavenger* was culled from his hot rod album *Checkered Flag*, which was produced by his father and Capital house producer, Jim Economides. It was his last national hit. The album did well locally as did his fourth Capitol album *Mr. Eliminator*, on which Economides brought in Gary Usher and his crew to try to inject a more contemporary sound.

Sadly nothing clicked nationally. Carl Belz summed up the problem best in his *The Story of Rock*. 'Dick Dale's popularity was based upon his live performances. These were electrifying, but their quality was not successfully transferred to his records. Capitol Records misinterpreted Dale's Southern California record sales, which were based upon memories of live situations.'

Although Dale never broke nationally, his local popularity became legendary. Writer Tom Wolfe commented on it in his *Esquire* magazine article, There goes (Varoom! Varoom!) that Kandy-Kolored Tangerine-Flake Streamline Baby.

Dick carried on regardless, making more records and beach movies, and even appeared on the Ed Sullivan Show, but ill health forced him into an early retirement. Maybe the final word should be left to James Monsour who told Derek Taylor in '65, 'Elvis was a fraud. The real King was Dick Dale.'

Capitol Records wasn't alone in acquiring a stable of surf groups. Bob Keene's Del-Fi label, for example, used the tag 'The Originators of Surf Music' and boasted Bruce Johnson, The Lively Ones and a host of lesser known groups supplied by independent producer Tony Hilder.

Hilder had started with Kent/Modern as an A&R man before forming his own label CT. Around this time he met Bruce Morgan (who had written some early Beach Boys waxings) and whose parents Hite and

Dorinda Morgan owned and operated a mastering and recording studio. Soon Hilder was recording a host of Californian groups such as The Revels with *Church Key*, The Sentinals with *Latinia* and Jim Waller and The Deltas' *Surfin' Wild* and either released them on his newly formed Impact label or leased the masters to a host of local labels.

The Sentinals were a good example of a non-Southern Californian–Californian surf group. Hailing from the coastal town of San Luis Obispo in Northern California, their sound had a Latin influence and *Latinia*, composed by group member Thomas Nunes, is a good example of their output. The group won the West Coast battle of the bands in Pismo Beach, and often appeared at The Rendezvous Ballroom. They followed up their popular *Latinia* with *Sunset Beach*, released on Del-Fi Records in January 1963.

Del-Fi was one of Hilder's biggest customers, although Bob Keene was never known for his generosity. For example, he paid Hilder a mere hundred dollars for the master of Dave Myers and The Surftones album *Hangin' Twenty* — studio time alone had cost Hilder fifty dollars. The group received nothing.

Jim Masoner of The Lively Ones also recalled a similar experience under the Keene regime. 'The group never received any royalties from our records,' he said. 'Not even the writing royalties. I made a mistake of putting The Lively Ones name down on the writing credits. Del-Fi was able to say they owned The Lively Ones name because of the contract and the fact that they owned the publishing company, they were able to take all the money. We were ripe to be taken advantage of, it was easy for them to do it. Hell, we were just a bunch of kids having a good time. We would gripe and complain a lot, but Del-Fi would just pacify us.'

The Lively Ones started life as The Surfmen, and comprised Ray Hunt, Tim Fitzpatrick, Joel Willenberg, Ron Griffith and Ed Chiaveirini. They cut Ray Hunt's *Paradise Cove* on the Titan label and it was released in January '62, becoming a sizeable local hit. Internal disputes led to Hunt leaving the group and being replaced by Jim Masoner. Carrying on under the same

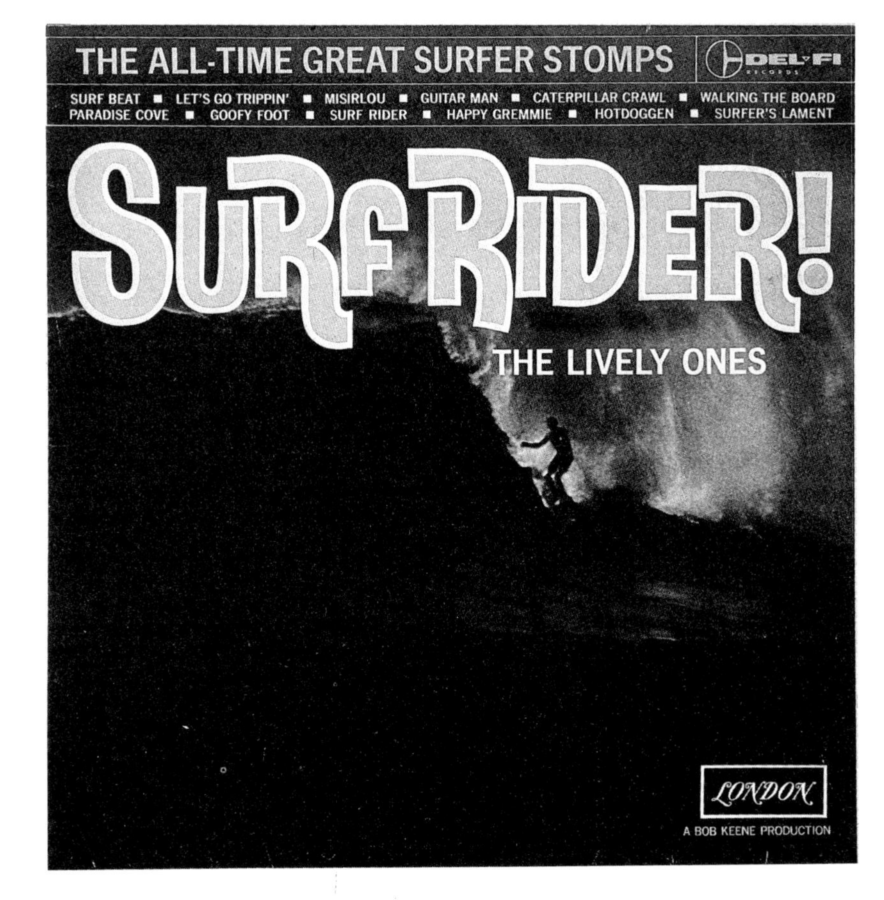

name, they made an appearance with KFWB disc jockey Gene Weed — as Ron Griffiths remembered. 'Gene liked what he saw and heard and was going to get us connected with Del-Fi Records later on. Anyway he thought that because we had changed guitar players and Ray Hunt, who was no longer in the group, had originally formed The Surfmen, then we should change our name.' They eventually agreed on the name The Lively Ones after a suggestion from Weed, and released *Guitarget* on the Del-Fi label in October '62.

The group had recorded their debut disc at the Sound House Studio in El Monte, and soon returned there to make their first album *Surf Rider*. Produced by Bob Summers, who also supplied two of the album's tracks *Hotdoggen* and *Surfer's Lament*, the album also featured sleeve notes by Gene Weed. 'For me to tell you The Lively Ones are good', he wrote, 'would be an understatement; these five young men from Orange County have found the Sound that is Surfin'.'

The album featured two original group compositions, *Goofy Foot* and *Happy Gremmie*, but undoubtedly the strongest tracks were their cover versions of Dick Dale's *Surfbeat*, *Let's Go Trippin'* and *Miserlou*.

A little later the group appeared with Dick Dale on a couple of shows and so impressed James Monsour that he asked them to back his son on a full-time basis. The group declined his offer as it would have meant dropping Masoner from the line-up.

The Lively Ones made four more albums and a handful of singles for Del-Fi but, like Dick Dale, their popularity made very little impact outside the Southern California area. The Pyramids from Long Beach, on the other hand, gained a national top twenty hit with their surf classic *Penetration*, and because of their bald heads even made the UK national press under the headline 'America's answer to The Beatles!' The group included Will Glover, Skip Mercer, Ken McMullen and Steve Leonard and became known as 'the crazies of the surf scene'.

Their album *The Original Penetration*, produced by John Hodge and Larry Wilson, fared well, as did their follow-up single, *Pyramid's Stomp*. They made their big screen debut in William Asher's *Bikini Beach* in '64.

Around this time they left Best (a Long Beach, California label) and signed to Cedwicke. Unfortunately, their two singles for the company, *Midnight Run* and *Contact*, failed to make the same impression as *Penetration*.

With the success of groups like The Pyramids, The Surfaris and The Chantays (the latter two groups are featured in a later chapter), surf groups began to spring up all over the US. The Astronauts from Boulder, Colorado and the Trashmen from Minneapolis made the national charts with surf-inspired numbers.

The Astronauts were a straight mid-west High School rock 'n' roll group until they contacted RCA's A&R Director, Steve Sholes. During an interview with Sholes in Hollywood, where two of the group's members Bob Demmon and Jim Gallagher played him their demo, he was interrupted by a phone-call from a distributor who informed him of the huge sales The Beach Boys were having with *Surfin' U.S.A.* He covered the phone with his hand, leant over the desk and asked Demmon and Gallagher if they played surf music, to which they replied 'Yes'.

In April '63 The Astronauts' Stormy Patterson, Rick Fifield, Dennis Lindsey, Gallagher and Demmon were back in Los Angeles recording their first album *Surfin' With The Astronauts* at the old NBC building on Sunset & Vine.

The album produced by Al Schmidt was basically a set of cover versions of some of



**Below: The Crazies of the surf scene, The Pyramids at Bikini Beach.**

the best known surf tunes of the day. Dick Dale's *Let's Go Trippin'*, The Beach Boy's *Surfin' U.S.A.*, The Chantays' *Pipeline* and The Marketts' *Surfer's Stomp* were all included, plus a group original *KUK* (which describes a non-surfer's problem of understanding the lingo), and finally three compositions from the pen of Lee Hazlewood: *Movin'*, *Batman* (also recorded by The Surfaris) and *Baja*.

Jim Gallagher: 'The session went fast because we had practiced hard before coming to California. One song that did give us trouble was *Miserlou* and it took thirty-three takes to get it down. Bob even played the trumpet on it. *Baja* and *Movin'* were pushed on us by Al Schmitt, who was good friends with Lee Hazlewood. Looking back, we were not sorry as *Baja* was our biggest hit.'

*Baja* coupled with *KUK* climbed into the hot hundred in July '63 as did The Trashmen's *Surfin' Bird* five months later.

The mid-West Trashmen comprised Tony Andreason, Dal Winslow, Bob Reed and Steve Wahrer. Drummer Wahrer penned *Surfin' Bird* and it was produced by Minneapolis record store owner, George Garrett and released on his Garrett label. However, Garrett Records was legally forced to surrender the copyright of *Surfin' Bird* to Beechwood Music in March '64. Beechwood claimed the song was copied from The Rivingtons' *Papa Oom Mow Mow* and *The Bird Is The Word* which they owned.

Unperturbed by the legal action, the group released the follow-up single *Bird Dance Beat* and the album *Surfin' Bird* which featured the dependable *Miserlou* and a cover of The Astronaut's *KUK*.

After *Baja* had become a national hit, The Astronauts' work-load trebled: movies, tours, TV appearances and more records. However, it really all started after they appeared as a warm-up act for a Beach Boys show.

Bob Demmon: 'We were really excited. We went to the Retail Clerks Hall in Buena Park to open for The Beach Boys. We got on stage and just blasted the kids and they loved us. After our set we stayed and listened to The Beach Boys. They were so bad that we left.'

Perhaps the early Beach Boys lacked the on-stage presence of a Dick Dale, but above all others they projected the Californian surf myth into the international record charts and, more importantly, survived well beyond it.

**Above: The land-locked Astronauts.**

# Surfurbia:
# *The Early Beach Boys*

*You don't have to go to the islands to have a lot of fun*
*Just pretend your patio's an Island in the sun.*

*Luau* — Bruce Morgan

**L/R Top: Mike Love and Brian Wilson; front row, Dennis Wilson, David Mark and Carl Wilson.**

**Los Angeles has been described as 'Nineteen suburbs in search of a City'. The Wilson brothers Brian, Dennis and Carl and their cousin Mike Love grew-up in one of these — Hawthorne.**

**Bordering the Pacific Ocean and sandwiched between Inglewood and Gardena, Hawthorne was very much a green and pleasant white middle-class portion of the post-war American Dream. The brothers' childhood wasn't too dissimilar to that of the popular TV series *My Three Sons*. It had all the ingredients: blue jeans, sneakers, apple pie, good old homespun philosophy and enthusiastic parents Murry and Audree Wilson.**

Murry Wilson had travelled west from Kansas during the Great Depression and had settled in Los Angeles. On June 20, 1942 Audree and Murry had their first son, Brian Douglas. Dennis Carl followed on December 4, 1944 and by the time they had Carl Dean on December 21, 1946 they had set-up home on West 119th Street in the South Bay suburb of Hawthorne. 'It was really weird,' Brian once recalled while cushioned behind a high security fence. 'We'd mow down the lawn and the lawn would taper into the street.'

Audree Wilson: 'Brian started singing when he was just a little bitty guy, three years old. He'd sing right on key. He loved to hear me play the piano, he loved the chords and he'd say, "Play that chord again".'

Brian started taking accordion lessons. After just six weeks his teacher commented to Audree 'I don't think he's reading. He hears it just once and plays the whole thing perfectly'. Surprising for a child who was deaf in one ear, the result of a childhood accident.

Music always played a big part in the Wilson's household. Apart from running a successful heavy machinery importing company, Murry was a part-time songwriter (Lawrence Welk played his *Two-step, Side-Step*) and would often sit at the piano with Audree singing duets.

Brian carried on his formal music training while attending Hawthorne High. 'Unfortunately,' as he recalled, 'I allowed my position on the Varsity baseball team and my involvement in a rock group called The Pendletons to distract from my music lessons . . . I stopped doing my assignments and ended up with a 'C' in the course.'

Dennis remembered an experience Brian had while in sixth grade. 'Brian used to sing in school. He sang very high and all his buddies that he'd hang out with laughed at him. He ran home from school, and I chased after him. It broke my heart to see him emotionally involved in the music at such an early age and have his friends laugh at him, call him a girl or something.'

While attending High School Brian became heavily influenced by rock 'n' roll: '*Rock Around The Clock* shocked me', he once said. 'I mean, I was so electrified by the experience — that song was really it.' His other great musical influence at the time was The Four Freshmen and he'd pick out the harmony parts of their records at the piano and practice singing them with his brothers and cousin Mike Love.

Carl was keen to learn to play the guitar and he started taking formal lessons in the backroom of a nearby accordion studio. Put off by the formality of the lessons — in his own words: 'I just wanted to rock' — he dropped out. A short time later he met a



**Below: The great inspiration.**

**Above: Brian and the group at a local High School sock-hop.**

young guitarist John Maus (of later Moon-gooners and Walker Bros. fame) who taught him, among other things, some Chuck Berry riffs.

One night, while on their way home from The Angeles Mesa Presbyterian Church Youth Club, Brian and Mike talked seriously about forming a group. Mike decided to take-up the saxophone, Dennis was talked into playing the drums and with Brian on piano and Carl an already competent guitarist, it wasn't long before they all began rehearsing together. Brian remembered that a fellow Cougar football teammate by the name of Al Jardine played stand-up bass and invited him along.

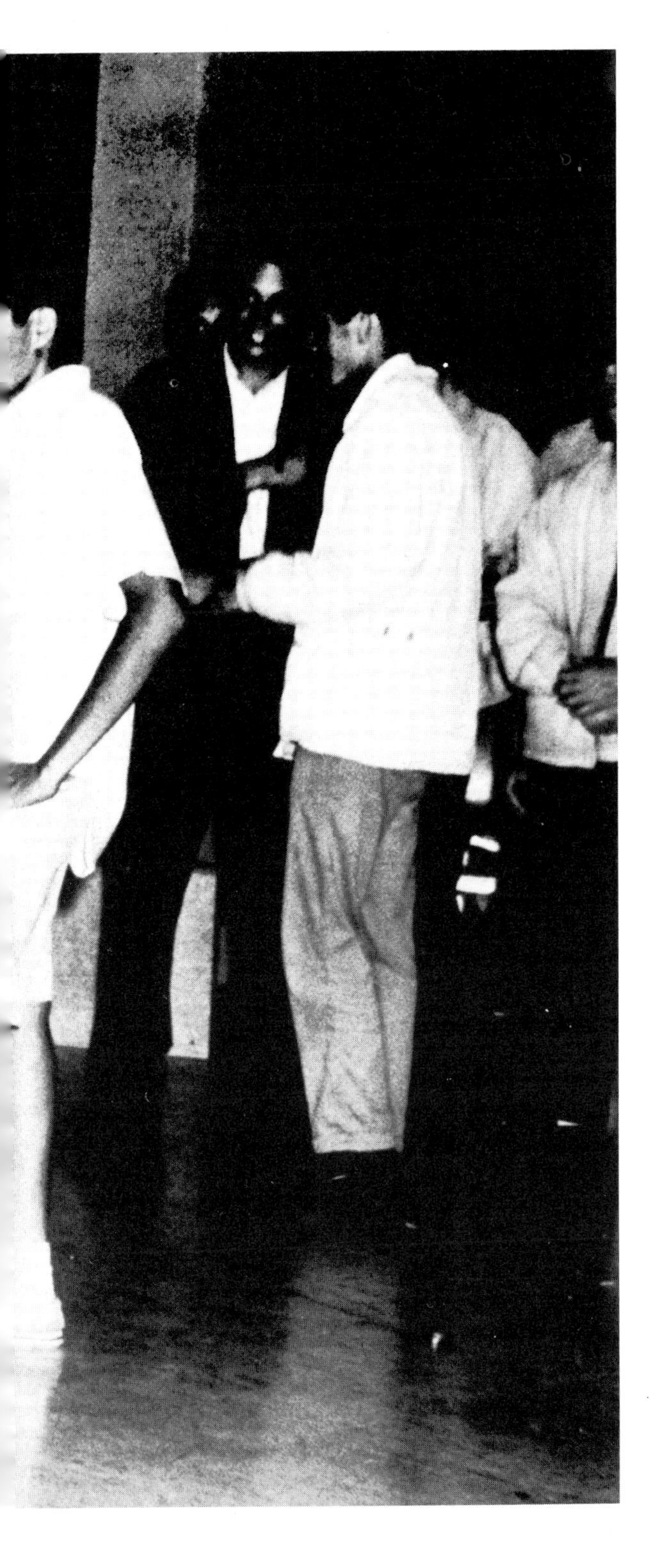

Al and Brian had become buddies after Al recovered one of quarterback Brian's fumbled pitch-outs and ended up with a broken leg for his trouble.

Al was more keen on folk music and The Kingston Trio in particular, but agreed to join Brian's rock 'n' roll combo.

During the summer of '61 the quintet got together and practiced playing a variety of tunes from *Duke of Earl*, *Barbara Ann* and *Johnny B. Goode* to a host of Everly Brothers and Four Freshmen songs. Their rehearsals would come to an abrupt halt at weekends. Dennis, equipped with his wax, board and woodie would head down the Pacific Coast Highway to his favourite surfin' spot off the Redondo Beach pier.

Mike, who was also something of an athlete (running track and cross country at Dorsey High) would often accompany him. One day while on their way home from the beach, Dennis and Mike first talked about the idea of writing a surf song.

They soon put the idea to Brian, and Dennis told his older brother that every morning they have surfing news on the radio, 'You know they tell you the best places to surf.'

"*Well, I woke up this morning, turned on the radio*
*I was checkin' out the surfin' scene to see if I would go.*"

Dennis wrote down a page of surfing terms and suggested that they write the song then and there. Mike worked up the lyric while Brian added a simple melody line and together they gave the sport its first song — and Brian's final school piano and harmony report card the unfortunate 'C'.

Fred Morgan, Brian's music tutor at Hawthorne High once reminisced on his student's poor showing. 'Brian was the most quiet one of the bunch in his class', he told Timothy White for *Crawdaddy* magazine, 'he was a nice boy and a good student and was fairly popular with his class mates because he had a good laugh. But I had to give a 'C' for the year because he did not do what he was supposed to do. He did not finish his harmony exercises for one thing. Most important, he did not write a sonata. Instead of writing a sonata he wrote a song called Surfin'.'

*Surfin' is the only life, the only way for me*
*Surf, Surf, with me.*

Brian graduated from Hawthorne High and attended El Camino Junior College. 'In college', he told a reporter in 1964, 'I took a music appreciation course. The teachers were one hundred percent against anything except operas, symphonies, cantatas, chamber and classical stuff. Well, I wasn't going to sit there and let any guy tell me that pop music is bad. I love both. After a year and a half, I became a college dropout and I'm not sorry.'

Murry and Audree Wilson were on vacation in Mexico City when Brian and Mike wrote *Surfin'*. When they returned they were greeted by the boys (who had spent the allowance their parents had left them on hiring musical instruments) and their new song. Audree was enthusiastic — Murry thought it crude. Not long after the holiday Murry was asked by his publisher Hite Morgan if he knew of anyone who could make a folk music demo. Murry suggested Al.

When Al turned up for the folk session he was accompanied by Brian, Carl and Mike and they pestered Morgan saying 'We've written a song about the surfing sport and we'd like to sing it for you'. Morgan agreed to hear it and after they had finished Dorinda Morgan (Hite's wife) called from the studio booth 'Drop everything, we're going to record your song. I think it's good.'



They cut *Surfin'* in two hours at the Morgan's single track studio with Al on double bass, Carl on guitar, Brian singing harmony while playing brushes on the drums and Mike singing lead vocal with a severe cold.

All five, now calling themselves The Pendletons (after a popular shirt surfers wore), turned up for the session that produced the disc's flip side *Luau*, an original song written by the Morgan's son Bruce.

It was now down to Morgan to secure a deal and he found it with Herb Newman's local Candix label. Newman loved the disc and wanted to release it immediately, but there was one problem — he didn't like the group's name. So he, Joe Saraceno and publicist Russ Reagan put their heads together and came up with the name The Beach Boys. To give the disc an added bit of interest they decided to release it on the newly formed X label and it appeared on December 8, 1961. Mike Love remembered: 'We didn't even know we were The Beach Boys until the song came out. It was that kind of thing. We could have said "No we're not going to be The Beach boys," but it sounded pretty far out.'

The disc was quickly switched to the Candix label and was played on three stations in LA every hour, twenty-four hours a day. *Surfin'* soon topped the local charts and climbed to number seventy-five in the national hot hundred.

The Beach Boys made their first public appearance with Dick Dale at The Rendezvous Ballroom and, as Dorinda Morgan recalled, 'Brian and Dennis had a little stage fright. Brian was a little perturbed by the crowd. The Beach Boys were not a smash there, but they weren't badly accepted, but they thought they were, especially Brian.' They faired better at the '61 New Years' Eve Ritchie Valens Memorial Concert held at the Long Beach Municipal Auditorium, where they performed three songs. The concert also marked Al Jardine's final live appearance with the group before leaving for college and a dental career.

February 8, 1962 found them back at Morgan's studio where they cut four new original compositions: *Surfin' Safari*, *Karate* (also known as *The Beach Boys Stomp*), *Judy* and *Surfer Girl*. The latter two written by Brian, were about his then girlfriend Judy Bowles. Around this time they also recorded two more Bruce Morgan songs. Dorinda Morgan: 'We put their voices on pre-recorded instrumental tracks of *Barbie* and *What a Young Girl Is Made Of* — both written by my son Bruce. We had wanted some more sides of them and Murry agreed that they owed us a couple . . . Dennis didn't come to those sessions, but Audree did. Audree is singing on those.' They had hoped that one of the tracks would be chosen by Candix as a follow-up single. Unfortunately, the label was going through some financial problems and later folded, but not before The Beach Boys received three hundred dollars royalties for *Surfin'*.

With the collapse of Candix it was left to Morgan and Murry Wilson (who had by this time become their fulltime managers) to trundle the demos around the major LA labels. Both Decca and Liberty had rejected the tapes when Al Jardine called it quits and Hite Morgan too became disenchanted.

A short time later a young LA songwriter by the name of Gary Usher introduced himself to the group, and he and Brian were soon collaborating on a number of new songs.

David Marks had replaced Jardine by the

time the group (using their *Surfin'* royalties) booked themselves into Western Studios to re-cut *Surfin' Safari* and a new Wilson/Usher song *409* — a hot rod song that perfectly complemented the surfin' tune.

Russ Reagan sent the *Safari* demo to Wink *Deck of Cards* Martindale who was a producer at Dot Records. Reagan later said 'Wink heard the record, loved the record and played it for his boss. His boss turned it down because he felt that surfing music was a flash in the pan.'

After the Dot rejection, Reagan suggested to Murry that he should go and see Nick Venet over at Capitol Records. So armed with the double-sided demo Murry found himself in the Capitol Tower office of producer Venet.

'Nick acted real cool', Murry Wilson once related. 'He said "You come back in an hour and we'll let you know if we want you to be Capitol recording artist."' After Wilson had left his office Venet rushed over to Voyle Gilmore's office, burst in and blurted 'Boss, I've got a double-sided smash for Capitol.' Capital pushed *409* as the A-side, arguing that surfing was just a local phenomenon. However, it soon became clear to them that they had made a mistake and flipped the disc. *Surfin' Safari* soon hit number fourteen in the national charts while *409* trailed at number seventy-six.

Around the time The Beach Boys double-sided hit was blazing up the charts, The Morgans leased *What Is a Young Girl Made Of* and *Barbie* to the local Randy Records label credited as Kenny and The Cadets . . . It sank into the world of pop trivia.

Unfortunately, The Beach Boys second Capitol single *Ten Little Indians* almost suffered the same fate. Chuck Britz their engineer at Western Recorders: 'When they signed with Capitol, Nick Venet wanted to do an album with *Ten Little Indians* . . . and that was the only bomb I know they had.'

*Ten Little Indians* did appear on their debut album *Surfin' Safari* along with the title track and *409*. Although the album became a top thirty hit it was not truly a surf record. Capitol, perhaps aware of this, dropped Brian's *Land Ahoy* (an early *Sail on Sailor*) in favour of leasing the Candix *Surfin'* hit.

For their next single Brian had the idea of

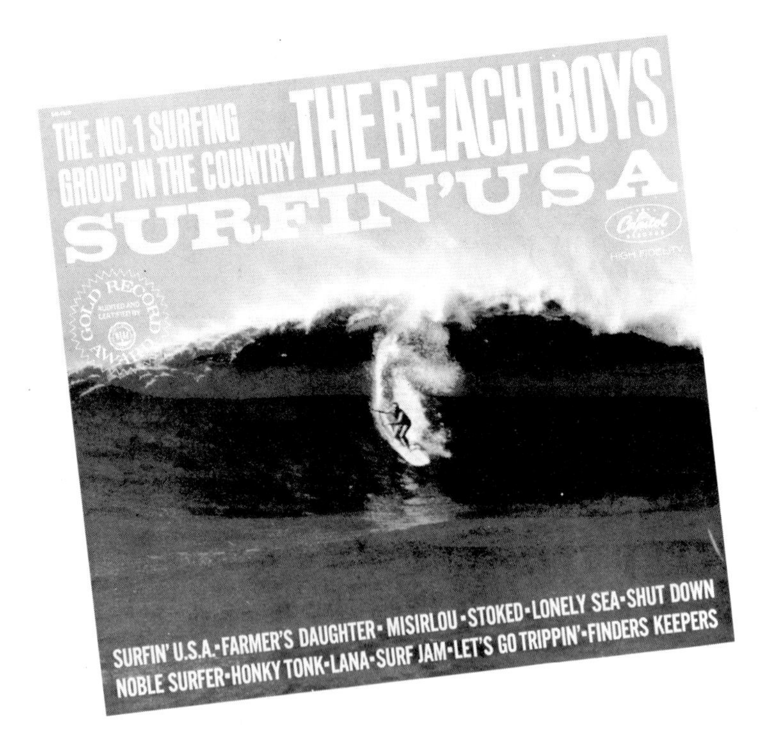


doing a Chubby Checker style song, and enlisted the help of Judy Bowles' brother Jimmy. Jimmy was a surfer and Brian asked him to write a list of all the favourite surfing spots. Brian then worked it up into a lyric and borrowing the melody line from Chuck Berry's *Sweet Little Sixteen* — *Surfin' U.S.A.* was born.

The disc became their biggest hit to date, reaching the number three slot in the country. For the flip side *Shut Down*, Brian called upon KFWB disc jockey Roger Christian to supply the necessary pit-stop poetry. It too became a top twenty hit in its own right. To capitalize on the success of the double A-side, Venet wanted to rush out an album as quickly as possible. Murry recalled the session: 'At Western Recorders I remember they stood and sang thirteen hours straight to get an album out. Sometimes they were too exhausted, I had to make them mad at me to get the best out of them.'

The album *Surfin' U.S.A.* was released in May '63 and the sleeve featured a surfing action pic by *Surfer* magazine publisher John Severson, and a strap line that proclaimed 'Surf's Up! Here come The Beach Boys No. 1 Surfin' Group in The Country' and judging by the albums' sales who could doubt it, it rose to number two in the national charts.

Soon surfin' groups were springing up all over the country. 'Even in places', as Nick Venet put it, 'where the nearest thing to surf is maybe the froth on a chocolate shake'. Together with Jan and Dean, The Surfaris and others, The Beach Boys music had sent America California dreamin'.

But back on the corner of Hollywood and Vine, things weren't all sunshine and hits at the Capitol Tower, for Brian couldn't get on with producer Venet. 'He didn't tell the truth to them', Murry recalled.

He'd say, "Brian be here at 2.00, we're going to master your record," and then he would do the mastering himself before Brian got there. What he did was outsmart Brian. So Brian came home one day and said "Goddamit Dad . . . go down and tell Capitol we don't want him anymore, he's changing our sound".'

Murry Wilson eventually played the heavy with Voyle Gilmore and Brian got his way. Capitol not only allowed him to record The Beach Boys without the impedence of an Artist's Representative, but equally importantly at any studio of his choice.

Brian the producer quickly started work on a new single and album. He had become increasingly influenced by Phil Spector's Wall of Sound and recruited some of Spector's best session men for the task. Studio musicians such as drummer Hal Blaine, guitarist Glen Campbell and keyboard player Leon Russell were among those employed.

Hal Blaine once noted 'We as older musicians appreciated Brian 'cause at the time, I did sessions with guys who were into big band stuff, not pop music. They used to say things like, "Now I don't want you to tune up because we gotta play rock and roll".'

For Brian's first outing as producer he reworked the earlier unreleased surf ballad *Surfer Girl*, this time adding a Four Freshmen inspired intro. Keeping to the successful formula of coupling a surf and hot rod song *Little Deuce Coupe* was chosen as the flip side . . . and again Brian asked Roger Christian to delve into his golden handbook of auto terminology for the necessary and, above all, accurate lyrics.

*She's ported and relieved, and she's stroked and bored*
*She'll do a hundred and forty with the top end floored*
*She's my Little Deuce Coupe, you don't know what I got.*

Albeit with all Brian's new found artistic freedom he still retained many doubts and fears as he once confided to Christian. 'I don't know how to tell Dennis that the drumming on Little Deuce Coupe isn't his.'

Christian replied reassuringly 'Brian, in the past when you haven't felt something was right, and let it go, you've lived to regret it. Dennis'll understand. He won't be very happy about it, but . . . everyone in the group really respects you and your opinions.'

Dennis may have felt a little hurt after Brian broke the news to him. But at least their fans at the time had no idea that anyone outside the group appeared on their records — for example during their live shows *Little Deuce Coupe* was performed as an illustration of how The Beach Boys went about making a record. Mike's introduction would enlighten the audience by saying 'We start with Denny on the drums' . . . leaving the group's ego intact.

On the other side of the track, *Surfer Girl* turned out to be Brian's most treasured recording; he thinks back on it as being 'spiritual' and has added: '*Surfer Girl* is my favourite Beach Boys song. I liked the melody and I liked the music. It was the first ballad we ever did. We did it without knowing how; it was the first time we ever did a song like that.' *Surfer Girl* rose to number seven in the national hot hundred while *Little Deuce Coupe* peaked at fifteen.

About this time Brian was completely hooked by production techniques and looked for other possible avenues to further his experiments with sound. One of the first projects that he undertook outside The Beach Boys was to produce his song *The Surfer Moon*, by Bob and Sheri, on Murry Wilson's self-owned Safari label. Bob and Sheri were Bob Norberg, an old college buddy, and his girlfriend Sheryl Pomeroy.

Bob later teamed with Brian and Dave Nowlan under the name The Survivors for the Capitol single *Pamela Jean* (a melody Brian also used for The Beach Boys' *Car Crazy Cutie*). Brian cut the track at Goldstar studios while the flip side, *After The Game* was recorded at home on a reel to reel tape recorder.

Norberg (or Norman as he was also known also co-wrote a number of songs with Brian including Bob and Sheri's *The Humpty Dumpty* and The Beach Boy's *Your Summer Dream* and *Keep an Eye on Summer*.

However, the group that took up most of Brian's spare production capacity at the time were the all-girl Honeys.

The Honeys featured Marilyn Rovell (soon to become Mrs Brian Wilson), her sister Diane and their cousin Ginger Blake (Sandra Glantz). With Brian at the mixing desk they recorded a string of surfettes including *Shoot The Curl*, *Surfin' Down The Swanee River* and *Pray For Surf*.

Both *The Surfer's Moon* and *Surfin' Down The Swanee* (re-worked as *South Bay Surfers*) appeared on The Beach Boys' first Brian Wilson-produced album *Surfer Girl*.

The album, released in October '63 rocketed straight into the national top ten and was without doubt the best album the group had produced.

Credit to Capitol, they were the first to acknowledge Brian's production ability via



**Below: A UK taster.**

this little memo; 'Capitol wishes to express its special thanks to Beach Boy Brian Wilson for producing what we consider to be the finest Beach Boys album yet.'

Apart from the title song and the aforementioned tracks, *Surfer Girl* featured a sparkling array of sunny up-beat surf and car songs including the refreshing *Catch A Wave.*

*Catch A Wave*
*and you're sittin' on top of the world.*

Above all it perfectly mirrored their special Southern Californian lifestyle through such teen anthems as *Surfer's Rule, Hawaii, Our Car Club, Little Deuce Coupe* and *In My Room. In My Room* surfaced again a month later as the flipside of *Be True To Your School* — a colourful celebration of campus life. Brian even enrolled The Honeys as cheerleaders (Rah-Rah — Push 'em back! Push 'em back! Way back! hold that line boys) and with its near wall of sound quality, the disc romped up the charts reaching number six. *In My Room* became a top twenty hit.

**Below: Bye, Bye, David . . .**

Principally this double-sided hit marked the group's first real departure from their topical world of ho-dads and hot rods.

During the summer months Capitol started exploiting the group's back catalogue, repackaging their early hits (along with others) on such compilation albums as *Chartbusters Vol. 1 & 2* and *The Big Surfin' Sounds.*

This area of record company marketing is on the whole universally accepted. However, Capitol in The Beach Boys' eyes, overstepped themselves by releasing a dubious hot rod collection under the title *Shut Down.*

The album's sleeve notes screamed 'You can almost smell the rubber burn!' and went on 'This is a romping, road-searing album that's titled after the current high-riding hit by The Beach Boys.'

That sort of outright exploitation the group found hard to swallow since the album only featured two of their tracks. The remaining programme (apart from four Super Stocks tracks) was a very odd assortment that included Robert Mitchum's *The Ballad Of Thunder Road* and The Piltdown Men's *Brontossaurus Stomp.*

So not wishing to go through the same experience again The Beach Boys released the *Little Deuce Coupe* album within two months of *Surfer Girl.* Almost overnight *Little Deuce Coupe* overshadowed the success of its predecessor, reaching number four in the album charts.

The *Shut Down* fiasco wasn't the only hiccup in the group's '63 career: rhythm guitarist David Marks made a mysterious exit and was replaced by old boy Al Jardine.

David's departure has, over the years, become even more of a conundrum mainly because no one can conveniently remember if he left by choice or not. One thing is for certain, although he was a competent guitarist, Brian never allowed him to sing on their records. When I asked Al Jardine in '66 what the story behind Mark's departure was he could only offer me the obligatory 'No Comment'. However, he once stated 'A year after I dropped out of the group, *Surfin' U.S.A.* and *Shut Down* had just come out. I got a call from Brian and he says "How'd you like to go on tour with the group again?".'

David Marks when questioned on the

subject could only remember the period after the break-up. 'After the split' he said, 'I wasn't sure what to do, so I saw a buddy I'd met through Carl, a drummer who was fooling around with a garage band at Hawthorne High. I walked in and said "Alright guys, I'm taking over! Gonna make you stars!" So we became Dave and The Marksmen, the first rock group to be signed to A&M. We recorded (discs included *Cruisin'* and *Kustom Kar Show*), went on tours of California, got airplay on all the local stations, met a lot of boss jocks — and didn't sell any records.'

Some years later, when questioned about Marks, Mike Love told reporters 'He is sorely neglected, and unjustly so, for he's a fine gentleman, a nice person, and he's studied classical music at a music school in Boston.'

Although Marks was last pictured with the group on the reverse side of the *Little Deuce Coupe* sleeve, it's unlikely he appeared on the album's new titles.

For apart from the earlier *409* and *Shut Down* hits, the album included a remix of *Be True To Your School* (without The Honeys) and a host of pure tuck 'n' roll auto songs such as *Cherry, Cherry Coupe, Car Crazy Cutie, Custom Machine* and *Ballad of Ole' Betsy*.

However, with the addition of *Spirit of America* and *A Young Man's Gone*, Brian showed once again his ability to keep pace, for just when other groups were beginning to explore the world of street and strip machines, he took the phenomenon beyond the automobiles and placed it firmly in the driver's seat.

The first song celebrated the heroism of speed merchant Craig Breedlove and his three wheeled 7,800 pound Spirit of America jet car.

The Bonneville Salt Flats had seen some strange things 'but the strangest thing yet was a jet without wings', while the second became a paean to the late teen screen idol James Dean, who tragically died at the wheel of his Porsche on his way to a race meeting at Salinas.

Musically, both titles indicated the direction Wilson was taking The Beach Boys sound. The harmonic arrangement and sympathetic lyric of the former song was a direct preview of the classic *Don't Worry Baby* and *A Young Man's Gone* gave a clue to the way Brian would later use the group's voices as instruments.

The Beach Boys saw the year out with the seasonal-sleigh bell hot rodder *Little Saint Nick*. But, the flip-side was even more interesting as Brian (perhaps harking back to his Angeles Mesa Presbyterian Church days) arranged and produced in an acapella rendition of *The Lord's Prayer* . . . perhaps a bit of divine foresight on the Rev Wilson's part.

For The Beach Boys along with the whole US pop scene needed all the help they could summon during '64 . . . The year of The Beatles and the great UK take-over. . . .

**. . . Happy Christmas, Al.**

# Be True to Your School: *The Surfaris, The Chantays and The Second Division*

*Nothing but winners now, you losers scram*
*I've got no time for a test or a schoolbook exam*
*Hot Rod High* — Gary Usher; Roger Christian

**Southern California's green lawned and asphalt High Schools were an ever present backdrop in the surf and hot rod era-school days and campus life was celebrated in a host of songs including *Pom, Pom Play Girl, School Is a Gas* and *The New Girl in School*. While many members of the surf crowd were still attending class when they recorded their biggest hits.**

Above all others, The Surfaris and The Chantays epitomized this unique aspect of surfdom . . . for these two High School groups not only gained local recognition but went on to international fame via two of surf's greatest instrumentals . . . *Wipe Out* and *Pipeline*. The Surfaris (Jim Fuller, Ron Wilson, Jim Pash, Bob Berryhill and Pat Connolly) hailed from the town of Glendora. Nestling below the San Gabriel Canyon, on route between Pasadena and San Bernadino, Glendora was a mere freeway's cruise to the ocean. All the Surfaris surfed and Bob Berryhill the group's rhythm guitarist even owned the woodie that served to transport the group's surfing and musical equipment. Bob originally met Jim Fuller (lead guitar) and Pat Connolly (bass guitar) at a 1960 Sellers High School talent show. However, they didn't join forces until two years later when all three were juniors at Glendora High.



They were soon offered a job to play at a Pomona Catholic High School sock-hop and when they arrived early to set-up their equipment and run through their repertoire, they were met by drummer Ron Wilson. 'We made our first public appearance at a local dance only six hours after we started practising together', Wilson once

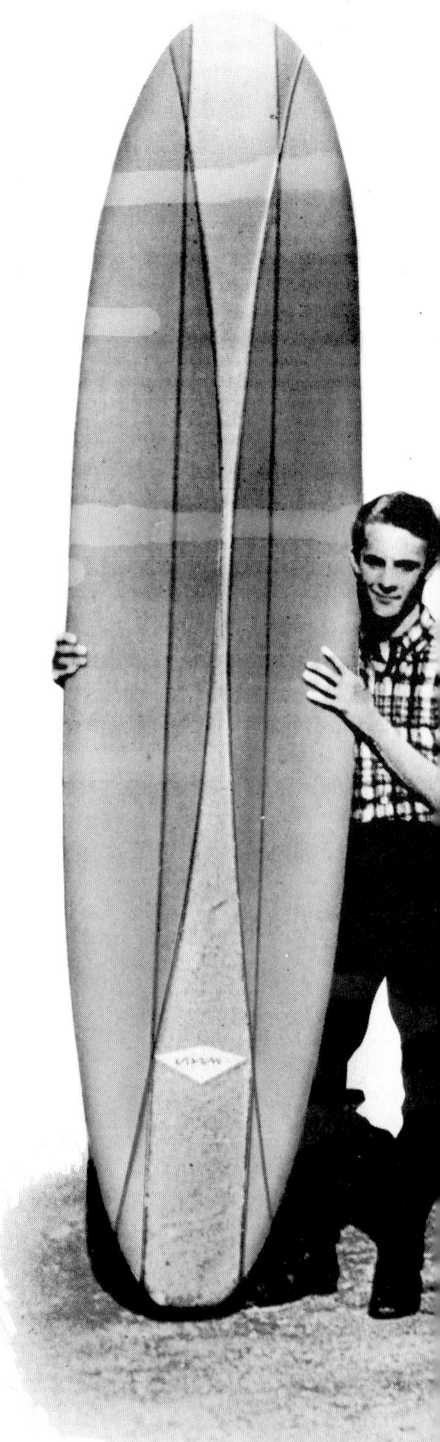

recalled. Ron, a senior at Charter Oak High also introduced the group to a young sophomore by the name of Jim Pash who played the sax. Two weeks later Jim joined the group and The Surfaris line-up was complete.

A short while later Ron Wilson had a dream during which he composed a song:

*Down in Doheny, where the surfers all go*
*There's a big beach blondie named Surfer Joe.*

The following day he played *Surfer Joe* to the rest of the group, after hearing it, they started looking at ways to record it. Dale Smallin a neighbourhood friend (who allowed the group to practice at his home) was appointed manager and he quickly organized a recording session at Pal Recording Studios in Cucamonga.

Pal offered the group four hours studio-time plus one hundred copies of the disc at the bargain price of $100.00.

The group and their parents put up the money between them, studio time was booked and the recording session was quickly underway. After completing *Surfer Joe*, Smallin asked the group if they had another original song for the flip-side, they didn't!

Jim Fuller put forward a twelve bar dittie entitled *Stiletto*, it sounded somewhere between the backbeat of Dick Dale's *Let's Go Trippin'* and a faster version of Duane

**Below: The Surfaris L/R Jim Fuller, Jim Pash, Ron Wilson, Bob Berryhill and Pat Connolly.**

Eddy's *Yep*. At least it was a start if not completely original.

Paul Bull and Dave Aerni, owners of Pal Studios (who as The Preston Epps found fame back in 1959 with *Bongo Rock*) suggested that Ron should work-up a drum cadence and have breaks between Jim's rhiff in much the same way as their *Bongo* hit.

This they did and Jim still selling his *Stiletto* title suggested that they should have the sound of a switchblade opening as an intro. The rest of the group thought it too punk and not in-keeping with their surfer boy image, so it was decided to give the instrumental a surfing title . . . they finally decided on *Wipe Out*. Albeit they still liked the idea of a sound effect intro and left it to Dale to produce the sound of a surfer being wiped-out. This he did by breaking a wooden roof tile into the microphone to get the crashing surfboard effect, and then injecting a hyena inspired laugh. Jim Pash: 'Dale had this crazy hobby. He used to practice chipmunk noises and witches cackling, and that's how we got the effect.'

With both tracks in the can, Smallin released the disc on his own DFS label (this version included two extra verses of *Surfer Joe*, plus an extra few seconds at the end of *Wipe Out*) and the group went proudly about selling their waxing to their school friends.

Small, not content with this small distribution network and feeling the group had a potential hit on their hands went in search of a more lucrative deal — a search that ended at the office of Richard Delvy.

Delvy had formerly been the drummer with The Belairs and after the group disbanded he formed The Challengers Surf Band with fellow ex-Belair Jim Roberts.

Using some of LA's finest session musicians Delvy, produced Valuts highly successful Challengers *Surfbeat* album. After the album's success he formed the Princess and Triumph labels while also acquiring the reputation of one of the West Coast's leading record industry hustlers. Also sensing the disc's hit potential Delvy agreed to release it on his Princess label.

Although *Surfer Joe* was the intended A-side, the DJ's started playing *Wipe Out* over the airwaves and it soon became a local hit, breaking first in Fresno, California. Delvy offered The Surfaris $5,000 for the rights of *Wipe Out* and *Surfer Joe*, Smallin thought it a great offer. However, some of the group's parents were less than enthused by the deal, so The Surfaris finally rejected it.

After their initial success on the Fresno charts the group were invited to perform at the town's Cinnamon Cinder — their first major gig, performing with such luminaries as The Righteous Brothers.

It wasn't long before they came to the attention of a major label and in April '63 Dot released *Wipe Out* coupled with *Surfer Joe* nationally.

The disc quickly rocketed to the number two position and Dot asked the group to cut an album. Richard Delvy and John Marascalo were appointed producers for the project and they gave The Surfaris a number of instrumentals to learn. These numbers mainly consisted of other instrumental hits including Sandy Nelson's *Teen Beat*, The Ventures *Walk Don't Run* and Booker T and The M.G.'s *Green Onions*.

However, little did The Surfaris know that Delvy had already cut the sides using his own group and it was The Challenger's versions that finally appeared on The Surfari's *Wipe Out* album — only the title track and *Surfer Joe* were by the original group.

Dale Smallin who had been in league with Delvy and Co. was fired, while law suits flew thick and fast resulting in cash settlements, sleeve changes and The Surfaris leaving Dot.

Unfortunately, the group weren't out of the white water yet, for another group calling themselves The Surfaris brought a suit against them in an attempt to stop them from using the name.

The Original Surfaris (Larry Weed, Charly Vehle, Jim Tran, Al Valdez, Mike Biondo and Doug Wiseman) as they would later be known, lost the case as the judge ruled that the Glendora group had become known nationally.

The Original Surfaris who hailed from the Fullerton/La Habra area of Los Angeles are probably best remembered for such instrumentals as *Moment of Truth*, *Surfari*, *Bombora* and *Midnight Surf*.

Once the dust had settled The Surfaris put their career in top gear, starting with a '63 appearance with The Beach Boys and The Pyramids at The Riverside Municipal Auditorium and climaxing with a new recording contract with American Decca. Their debut single for American Decca was another group original, *Point Panic* coupled with Jim Fuller's *Waikiki Run*. Released in September '63 it quickly rose into the national top fifty and as on *Wipe Out*, *Point Panic* also included a manic intro from Dale Smallin — his last appearance on record.

On the international front the group were attracting fans from as far afield as Australia and Great Britain. In the UK for example their sound was picked up by the Mods, *Wipe Out* was used to introduce the weekly pop show *Ready, Steady, Go*, while groups like the Cardiff based Surfbeats covered their songs. The late Keith Moon once told me that The Who had based their powerhouse instrumental *The Ox* on The Surfaris *Waikiki Run*.

Back in the recording studio they set to work on a new album, this time with veteran producer Charles 'Bud' Dant — the resulting album *The Surfaris Play* also gained a high chart placing.



**Below: The original—unoriginal Surfaris album.**

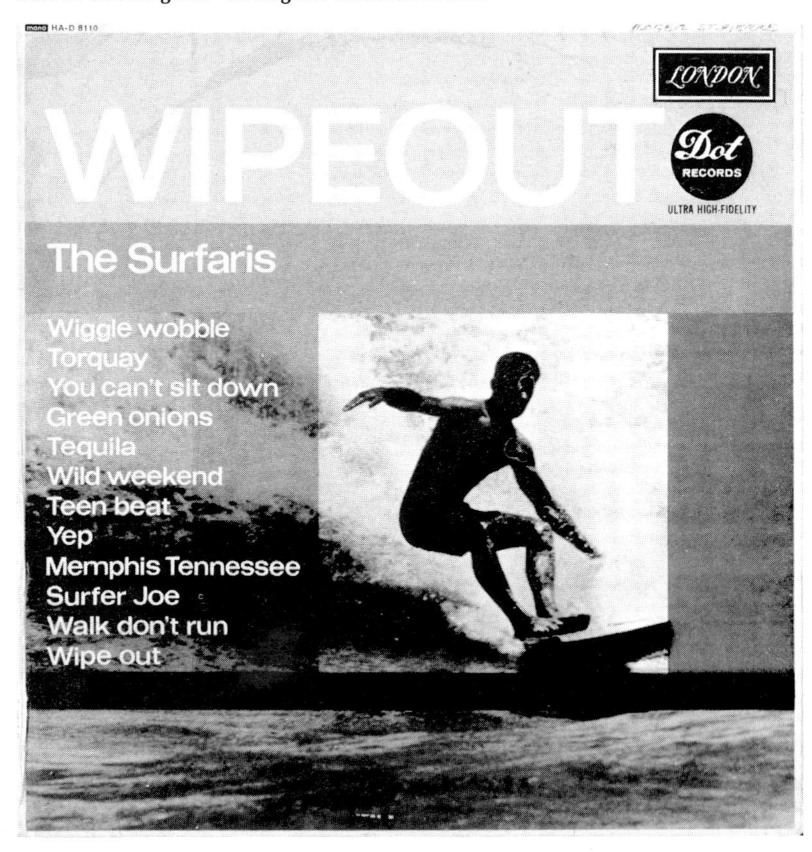

Owing to the fact that American Decca under the label Brunswick was distributed in the UK by Decca Records (who still listed the Dot *Wipe Out* album in their catalogue) the group's re-working of *Wipe Out* — without the Smallin intro — and *Surfer Joe* were dropped from the UK *Surfaris Play* in favour of their cover version of The Astronauts *Baja* and *Blue Surf* another group original.

The forementioned tracks have yet to see daylight in the US. The rest of the album, apart from Leiber and Stollers *I'm A Hog For You* was pure surf — from Dick Dale's *Surfing Drums* and *Miserlou* to their own *Surf Scene* and *Surfaris Stomp*. During term time the group had to restrict their appearances to in and around their hometown, although during the summer '63 recess The Surfaris managed to fit in a major tour of Hawaii. Jim Pash: 'While staying at the Waikiki Grand, the group would go up to the twentieth floor and drop their water glasses down into the swimming pool and later go diving for them without anyone knowing' . . . little devils.

**The British connection: *The Surfaris Play UK* sleeve and below the Welsh Surf Beats.**

The Surfaris saw the year out with two more singles, the seasonal *A Surfer's Christmas List* — a woesome tale of a surfer who loses his board at Point Panic — coupled with *Santa's Speed Shop* and the hot rodding *Scatter Shield*. The flip-side of *Scatter Shield, I Wanna Take A Trip to the Islands* was a new Ron Wilson surf song and featured The Honeys on backing vocals.

*Everybody's comin' and we're gonna have a ball*
*We're gonna take a trip to the Islands.*

*I Wanna Take A Trip to the Islands* became a big hit for them in Australia and January '64 found the group on the three week Surfside '64 tour of Australia and New Zealand.

The package also featured The Beach Boys, Roy Orbison and an Australian surf group The Joy Boys. John Bogie of The Joy Boys, 'Dennis Wilson, the young drummer with The Beach Boys, and The Surfari's drummer Ron Wilson all used the one drum kit on The Surfside '64 tour. Well the drum kit was actually Dennis's and it was a Rogers. To own a kit of Rogers in those days was magic. Anyway, the kid from the Surfaris used to use the butt ends when he did the cymbal crash and here was Dennis who prided himself in that he had Buddy Rich personally pick out his cymbals and here was Ronny using the butt ends of his heavy drum sticks on them. It all came to a head when we were over in New Zealand and Ron came up with a wack into a cymbal off one of the drums and the whole cymbal disintegrated and all that was left was the little bell on the top. Dennis just stood there in the wings saying "I'm gonna kill that guy" and shaking his fists. But really The Surfaris as a whole were quite mad.'

At an Australian press conference Ron Wilson was asked his opinion on the tour so far and Australia in general 'Boy!' he replied, 'does your traffic get me down. I have to stop and think real hard before I cross the street, and as for driving in Sydney — I'd probably be killed in the first five minutes.' When they were questioned about their recent musical change from surfin' to hot rod, Clay Hentey their road manager answered, 'Hot-roding music is basically the same as surfing music — only the lyrics are different — so I believe the surfing sound will be around for quite a

long time.' On their return to the States, they went straight back into the studio to put the finishing touches to their second Decca album *Hit City '64*. Apart from the inclusion of the *Scatter Shield/I Wanna Take a Trip to the Islands* single, the only new original to feature on the album was the *Wipe Out-ish Mystic Island Drums*.

The rest of the *Hit City '64* programme included cover versions of some excellent but little known surf instrumentals — from Aki Aleong and The Nobel's *Hiawatha* and *Earthquake* to Gene Mole's *Scratch*, on the vocal front Ron Wilson sang *Little Deuce Coupe* in his own inimitable style while little Jim Fuller was called upon to deliver an almost soulful *Louie Louie*.

To complete the album Charles Dant once again called upon The Honeys to help fill out the sound on *Be True to Your School* which they did in much the same way as The Beach Boys, while Gary Usher and his crew complemented The Surfaris sound on the Usher/Christian *Wax Board And Woodie* and Jimmy Gilmor's *Sugar Shack*. Released in February '64 *Hit City '64* for the most part worked very well and like its predecessor found a placing in the lower reaches of the national charts.

What with The Surfside tour, a new album and a BMI Achievement Award — 1964 found The Surfaris in a strong position, all that was needed now was a hit single . . . The first single of '64 was released

**A scene from *The Lively Set* (1964).**

in March and featured *Murphy the Surfie* — a surf instrumental they had picked-up from the Australian Joy Boys. It seemed a good choice as *Surfer* magazine ran the popular Rick Griffin cartoon strip under the same name. However, it was the flip-side *Go, Go, Go, for Louie's Place* that became the big regional hit for them. *Louie's Place* had a good time party feel, reminiscent of the later *Beach Boys Party* album and included plenty of hand-clapping and a girl group (probably The Honeys) giggling and generally joining in the fun.

The songs backbeat had started life as The Surfaris version of *Watermelon Man*, but after listening to the playback Charles Dant decided to re-work the arrangement and add a lyric and it was then given to Ron and Jim to sing it as a duet.

*Got a big date, with my baby tonight*
*Go, Go, Go for Louie's Place.*

Sadly *Louie's Place* failed to gain a national chart placing, so it was back to the studio for their second single outing.

This came via a Terry Melcher/Bobby Darin hot rod song *Boss Barracuda*, this recording gained an extra shot in the arm by being featured in the hot rod movie *The Lively Set* (1964).

Produced by Universal Pictures the movie starred James Darren, Pamela Tiffin, Doug McClure and drag racing's Mickey Thomas. Directed by Jack Arnold, it included newsreel footage of the Bonneville speed meets spliced between the main plot, while The Surfaris and *Boss Barracuda* could be heard (but not seen) over a poolside scene. Released in November '64, the flip-side featured another Jim Fuller instrumental *Dune Buggy*. Unfortunately, even with the help of *The Lively Set* exposure it too failed to make the big charts. Their third single of '64, the Usher/Christian's *Hot Rod High* coupled with *Karen* was released in October to coincide with the release of their latest album *Fun City U.S.A.*

*Fun City U.S.A.* produced by Charles Dant turned out to be probably their best ever album and even incorporated a sleeve note from Roger Christian, 'A little over a year ago,' he wrote, 'I was asked to MC a high school dance in the Los Angeles area. There were many acts featured that night, but it was plain to see that everyone had come to watch only one group. You guessed it, The SURFARIS. Until this time, I had heard a great deal about The SURFARIS' singing and playing, but had never caught their act myself. Now I was introducing them, and saying nice things about them to the audience, as they plugged in their amps; getting ready to tear it up. While they began to captivate the audience and myself, I then knew why this group was on top, whether they played Surf, Hot Rod, Rock or for slow dancing.'

Apart from the already released *Dune Buggy*, *Murphy the Surfie*, *Hot Rod High* and *Louie's Place*, the album included a sparkling array of goodies from Jim Fuller and Pat Connolly's vocal duet on Presley's *Hound Dog* (which also featured Pat's bass taking over the lead in the instrumental break) to the three new group instrumentals *Hot Rod Graveyard*, *Big Surge* and *Burnin' Rubber*.

Most reviewers agree, however, that the best track on the album (and the one that should have been released as a single) was the group's re-working of The Gambler's *Moon Dawg* — a sophisticated arrangement packed with reverb and space sound effects. Although their *Hot Rod High/Karen* single failed to make it big in the US *Karen* reached the number two position in of all places Japan.

*Karen* had been written by the Mosher–Marshall team as the theme song for the Universal Pictures television series *90 Bristol Court* — a Beach Boys version was finally chosen for the show, albeit, they never released it on record.

Gary Usher picked up on the song and produced The Surfaris version using Chuck Girard and Joe Kelly on background vocals. With this unexpected Japanese hit behind them they were invited to tour the country, this they did playing several concerts and TV shows. It was also reported that when not performing Ron Wilson could be found skateboarding around the streets of Tokyo.

On their return from the East they found that Gary Usher had been appointed staff producer at Decca Records and had his own ideas about the group's recording career. As will be revealed in the Surf City chapter, *Fun City U.S.A.* turned out to be the last *real* Surfaris album.

Two decades later Tom Hibbert wrote in his *The Perfect Collection* 'Fun City U.S.A. — Probably the best of the U.S. surfing instrumentalists on probably their best LP. Where the Ventures were weedy and the Chantays inconsistent and non-prolific, the Surfaris kept their woodys afloat for months.'

It should be pointed out that The Ventures weren't a bona fide surf group but already established recording stars picking-up on the surf music fad for a one off album in much the same way as Bo Diddly, Chubby Checker, The Shadows and a host of others. The Chantays, Brian Carman, Bob Marshall, Warren Waters, Ron Spickard and Bob Welsh on the other hand were . . . bona fide.

The Chantays, like The Surfaris started their musical careers while still attending high school. Warren Waters (bass) and Bob Spickard (lead guitar) were classmates at Santa Ana High School when they decided to form a group. They soon enlisted the help of fellow classmates Bob Marshall (piano) and Brian Carman (guitar). Brian also played a little sax — his brother Steve played saxophone with the Rhythm Rockers, a local surf band who recorded such surf unforgettables as *Foot Cruising* and *Rendezvous Stomp* — and were a great inspiration to the group.

They had already tried out a couple of drummers until they decided on the inexperienced but enthusiastic Bob Welsh. After practising together for a few months, they began appearing at local dances, starting by filling-in The Rhythm Rockers rest breaks. Although their repertoire at the time consisted of rock standards such as *Runaway* and *Riders In the Sky*, they became increasingly interested in surf music and Dick Dale in particular. Bob Spickard: 'I can remember the first reverb unit I ever played through. It was Dick Dale's and we used it without Dick ever knowing about it. Rob Marshall's father was in electronics and knew someone at Fender Instruments. He was able to borrow Dick's reverb unit, which was in for service at the time, for a few days. We were so impressed with this new gadget that Brian and I took our share of the profits from a dance and each of us bought one.'

Brian and Bob had been working on a

rhiff they had originally called *Liberty's Whip* and then *44 Magnum*, however, after seeing a surf movie featuring the notorious Hawaiian Pipeline they decided to call their tune *Pipeline*.

They were soon discovered playing at a dance at Big Bear (overlooking Lake Arrowhead) by KXFM radio DJ Jack Sands.

Sands quickly organized a recording session at Pal Recording Studios, Cucamonga, where the group recorded their latest composition *Move It* — a semi-vocal number coupled with *Pipeline*.

After trundling the demo around the major LA labels Sands finally secured a deal with Downey Records — with only one clause, that The Chantays re-record their waxing at Downey's own studio.

Downey Records had recently had a sizeable hit with The Rumblers *Boss* — distributed nationally by Dot, *Boss* crept into Billboard's top hundred and the company were looking to capitalize on their success.

The Rumblers, Mike Kelishes, Johnny Kirkland, Wayne Matteson, Bob Jones and Adrian Lloyd (who later left to form Adrian & The Sunsets) hailed from Norwalk, California and followed their *Boss* success with *Boss Strikes Back, Bugged, Angry Sea (Waimea)* and *It's A Gas* unfortunately without the same success.

Downey released The Chantays *Move It* in December '62 and it started moving up the local charts — that was until the jocks flipped the disc and by February '63 *Pipeline* was at the top of the Californian charts.

As with *Boss* and The Surfaris, *Wipe Out* Dot Records distributed the disc nationally and by March '63 *Pipeline* made the national top five. In the UK it became a top twenty hit while in Australia they were awarded the Pop Star of the Year Gold Disc by *Everybody's* magazine for capturing the number one slot for four consecutive weeks. Back home in California (limited by their schooling) they played everywhere from The Rendezvous Ballroom to the *Lawrence Walk* TV show.

Their debut album *Pipeline*, produced by Art Wenzel was fairly pedestrian, while its sleeve design must rate as one of the most boring in the history of rock music. Apart from the title track, there are only two tracks worthy of a mention, *Banzai* credited to Jack Sands and Bob Spickard's *El Conquistador*.

Riding on the success of its title the album did reasonably well, unlike their follow-up single *Monsoon* coupled with *Scotch Highs* which failed to make a national chart placing.

The poor chart showing of *Monsoon* wasn't the only problem The Chantay's

**Below: The Chantays.**

were facing, unhappy with their business affairs they fired Jack Sands on the grounds of mismanagement.

Back in the studio, again under the production auspice of Art Wenzel they cut their second and last album *Two Sides of The Chantays. Two Sides* was a far more satisfactory outing featuring as it did a vocal side, including *Move It*, while its flip-side was completely instrumental.

Their third single the instrumentals *Space Probe* coupled with *Continental Missile* were culled from the album and like the album itself failed to make any great impression on the charts.

Undaunted by their lack of chart action, The Chantays spent the summer of '64 touring Hawaii.

Prior to the tour, Bob Welsh quit the group to attend University and was replaced by drummer Steve Kahn. While on tour they performed at The Honolulu International Center, Yoko's The Waikiki Shell and made numerous TV and Radio appearances. One of the highspots of the tour was a surfing trip to the Pipeline: Bob Spickard; 'Although we just rode the eight foot white water, it was still exciting to see the twenty foot tubes of Pipeline.'

Sadly, the tour marked the end for the group, Waters and Carman quit and their fourth single died a very peaceful death.

Hot on the heels of The Surfaris and The Chantays were a number of aspiring high school surf groups, some of them such as The Crossfires and Jim Messina and The Jesters would have to wait until the mid-sixties before real fame would finally arrive.

The Crossfires started life as The Nightriders, a pure instrumental combo and played local high school hops in and around the Westchester area of Los Angeles, where most members attended school. The group was formed by Howard Kaylan (real name Kaplan) and Al Nichols and soon included Chuck Portz and Don Murry. By the time they had acquired Mark Volman, the group had changed their name to The Crossfires, and had started playing bigger gigs.

Volman: 'Our favourite handbill read: The Lively Ones, Eddie & The Showmen and another band for dancing — We were another band for dancing.'

However, they were soon signed to Capco Records (a subsidiary of ex-Teddy Bear Marshall Lieb's LA based Marsh label) and their debut single *Dr. Jekyll & Mr. Hyde* coupled with *Fiberglass Jungle* was released late in '63.

The flip-side made the number three position on Inglewood High's student top ten and that was about the extent of the disc's success.

As the surf instrumental genre grew, thanks mainly to the high school bands, more established acts jumped on the surf woodie; Jack Nitzsche gained a top forty hit with *The Lonely Surfer* in August '63.

While Duane Eddy took *Your Baby's Gone Surfin'* into the hot hundred the same year and Bo Diddley, The Ventures and even the UK Shadows had instrumental surf albums released. Albeit, The Shadows album had really nothing to do with surf music, their originals were covered by such surf groups as The Surfaris, The Challengers and The Sandells among others. Perhaps, out of all the surf music impersonators, The Ventures (being at least based on the West Coast) were better placed to cope with the surf boom — and gained a huge hit with their '63 *Surfing* album. Released on Dolton Records, it featured among its programme a cover of the English duo (ex-Shadows) Jet and Tony's *Diamonds* plus The Chantays *Pipeline*.

Feeling the vitality of the latter, they used a similar arrangement to up-date their 1960 hit: *Walk Don't Run* re-titled *Walk Don't Run '64*, the single with its Chantays feel — shot straight into the top ten.

However, the real credit for the popularity of surf instrumentals must fall to the young high school hit-makers, who, along with The Beach Boys and Jan and Dean, prompted writer Gus Kuhns in '63 to observe 'The sport of surfing had gained national recognition through feature motion pictures and popular "surfing" tunes on all the nation's juke boxes. In some areas, the surfboard had replaced the hot rod as a teenage symbol. Youngsters across the nation wear "makaha" T shirts and tennis shoes and peroxide their hair in order to have that sundrenched surfer look while they gyrate to rock-and-roll tunes. All that the people who live in landlocked portions of the United States needed were waves — they had already become surfers at heart.'

# Surf City: *Two Acts for Every Label*

*I've got a tank full of gas and I'm really gonna move*
*down to the beach where the surfers all groove*

*Wax Board and Woodie* — Gary Usher/Roger Christian

**Individually or as a team, Gary Usher and Roger Christian were two of the most productive, successful and overlooked musical talents of the surf hot rod era. They worked with, or supplied songs for, every act on the surf scene including The Beach Boys, Jan and Dean, The Surfaris and The Hondells among many others — and without a doubt each group benefited enormously from their highly perceptive output.**

This creative partnership quickly built a reputation and track record for capturing every Southern Californian teen fad of the day — providing many acts with just the right material to perpetuate the myths and sunlit fantasies that surrounded their West Coast teenage lifestyle.

Gary got his first break as a singer songwriter via the Lancet Label who released his *Tomorrow* coupled with *Lies* about the same time as The Beach Boys were topping the local charts with *Surfin'*.

His uncle (Benny Jones) lived in the same neighbourhood as the Wilson Brothers and while on a visit with his inlaws, Uncle Ben suggested that he should go over to the Wilson house and introduce himself. Usher: 'I went over and talked to them, they were practising, you could hear them all over the neighborhood — I seemed to hit it off with Brian right away; I seemed to have a soul affinity with him. We could touch each other on inner levels, even though neither of us knew anything about it at the time or how to do it.' Their meeting took place on a Sunday afternoon in January '62 and by the evening (over hot fudge sundaes) Gary and Brian were aleady writing songs together. Brian Wilson: 'He kind of showed me the spirit of competition — sorta showed me how to write songs — He was very creative.'

The first song they penned was *The Lonely Sea* (later to surface on The Beach Boy's *Surfin' U.S.A.* album). Usher: 'The first day I went over there, we wrote together. I played a little rhythm guitar and a little bass, not much and Brian played interesting piano. He knew all the progressive progressions.' *The Lonely Sea* took Brian and Gary just twenty minutes to write and they were soon back together collaborating on a host of new songs including

the tune that started the whole West Coast hot rod music craze . . . *409*;

*When I take her to the drags, she really shines*
*Giddy up, Giddy up, 409.*

It was Gary who came up with the idea of basing a song around his favourite Chevy engine while cruising around town with the Wilson brothers. Gary Usher: 'We'll do a thing, a giddy up, giddy up, meaning horses for horsepower. We were just kidding around. We came back and put it to three simple chords and it became a million-dollar craze.'

Beach Boy Mike Love: 'I can still remember being outside the Wilson house in Hawthorne. It was like two a.m. and here we got a tape recorder out on the lawn and peeling rubber, just dragging down the street, was this "409" O-boy! Neighbors calling up and coming out yelling "Shut Up!" It was a trip. We needed the sounds Y'know.'

Soon after Gary accompanied Murry Wilson and the group to Western Recorders to record a more polished version under the supervision of engineer Chuck Britz. Apart from *Surfin' Safari*, *409* became the major ingredient that secured The Beach Boys their Capitol Records contract.

Later, Gary also signed to Capitol and released his first single for the company *The Beetle* coupled with *Jody* while he also carried on co-writing with Brian on a part-time basis. Their partnership went on to produce a number of Beach Boy's favourites including the sensuous *Pom, Pom Play Girl*, the wistful *We'll Run Away* and the prayer-like *In My Room*;

*There's a world where I can go and tell my secrets to*
*In my room, in my room.*

The song was originally released as the flip-side of The Beach Boys *Be True To Your School* and eventually made it to the number 23 position in its own right.

Apart from their songwriting partnership Gary and Brian became close friends and it was Usher who introduced Brian to Marilyn Rovell . . . his future bride.

Diane Rovell: 'My cousin Ginger was dating Gary Usher and he was friends with Brian, and he came over one night and said, "I want to take you to see this group called The Beach Boys." They were at a place called Pandora's Box in Hollywood.' Aware of fifteen year old Marilyn in the audience, Brian asked her for a sip of her chocolate drink and accidentally spilt it over her blouse. After the incident, Gary formally introduced the couple and they quickly formed a romantic attachment. Brian was also pleased to learn that Marilyn her sister Diane and cousin Ginger were a singing group calling themselves The Honeys.

Diane Rovell: 'We got the Honeys from "early in the morning we'll be starting out/ some Honeys will be coming along" (from *Surfin' Safari*). Honeys were female surfers or the surfers girlfriends.'

The Honeys were originally known as The Rovell Sisters and consisted of Marilyn, Diane and Barbara Rovell. They first performed publically on television singing commercials and even won a number of local talent shows before Barbara dropped out to be replaced by their cousin Ginger Blake (Sandra Glantz).

Marilyn Rovell: 'Brian heard us sing and just flipped and said, "I've gotta cut with you".' He soon did, unfortunately without any great chart action.

At this time Gary seemed to have his finger on the pulse of the West Coast record industry and was soon introducing Brian and the group to a number of other music biz people. One such personality — singer/ guitarist Richie Burns once remarked 'Without Gary Usher there would have been no Beach Boys. Gary nurtured The Beach

Left: Gary Usher in the studio.

Boys; he brought them along, rehearsed with them and he brought them over to my house in Burbank and they would sit there, like little kids and say "Gee Gary, will we ever be as good as those guys?"' He continued. 'The only things they could sing good was material by The Four Freshmen and The Hi-Lo's. They could sing that stuff beautifully.

Gary was the one who worked with them and really convinced them to use today's lyrics and combine them with that sound.'

However, there was another guy that really clicked with Brian at this point ... KFWB disc jockey Roger Christian. Gary took Brian over to the station one night, just after midnight when the DJ was coming off the air. The two immediately struck-up a rapoire and were soon spending late nights talking and creating songs.

Apart from being a popular LA DJ Christian had gained a popularity and some recognition for his self-created commercials plugging the local drag strips and soon earned the tag 'Poet of the Strip'.

This insight into the world of hot rods and dragsters was just the right ingredient Wilson needed. Brian: 'Roger was really . . . really a guiding light for me. I'd go over there, see . . . he'd get off at midnight, OK, he'd do a night-time radio show from 9 to 12 every night and we'd go over to Otto's, order a hot fudge sundae and just . . . Whew! talk and talk.

We'd be writing lyrics ... hussling, y'know and all of a sudden we'd realize we'd written fifteen songs.' Indeed the two soon churned out a host of auto sagas starting with *Shut Down*:

*It happened on the strip, where the road is wide*
*Two cool shorts standing side by side*

The song was released as the flip-side of *Surfin' U.S.A.* and became a top twenty hit under its own steam or possibly fuel injection. Christian eventually added his pit-stop poetry to another eight Beach Boy standards including *Little Deuce Coupe*, *Car Crazy Cutie*, *Spirit of America* and the classic *Don't Worry Baby*:

*She makes me come alive and makes me want to drive*
*When she says, "Don't worry baby everything will come out alright."*

Jan Berry (of Jan and Dean) flipped when he heard *Shut Down* and by the end of the duo's career Christian was credited with over thirty J and D songs.

On at least one occasion his dedication for the precise and accurate lyric almost found him in deep water . . . legend has it that one night after his late KFWB show he decided to check out the correct street sequences for Dead Man's Curve — he passed me at Doheney etc when a blue light flashed and he was pulled over, suspected of kerb-crawling.

On less hazardous ground he discovered his *Little Old Lady From Pasadena* while watching a Dodge TV commercial, although he was later sued for the song. Christian also released his own singles, one of his early attempts being a seasonal novelty *Merri Christmas* coupled with *The Meaning of Christmas* for the Rendezvous label. Then shortly after The Beach Boys *Shut Down* hit, Roger released his own auto single *Big Bad Hodad* coupled with *The Last Drag*, unfortunately it failed to take the flag.

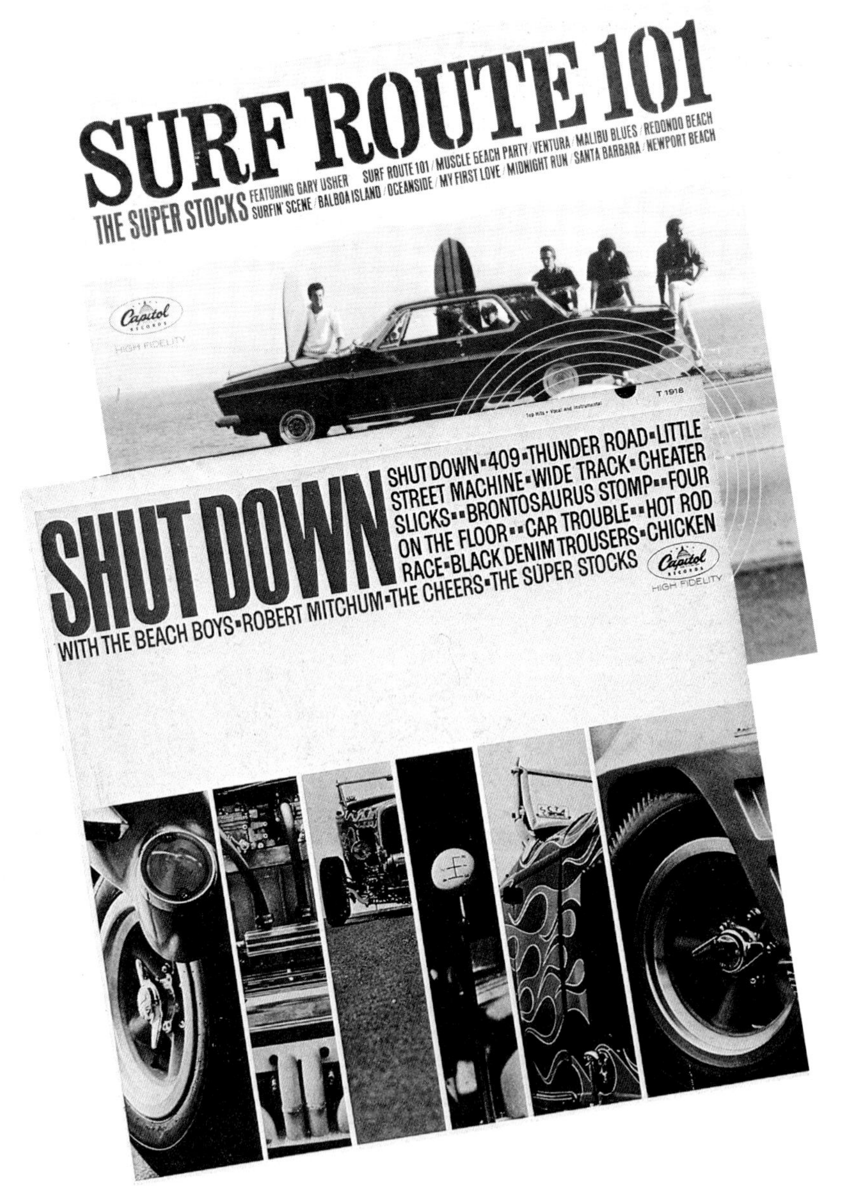


As Gary Usher's involvement with The Beach Boys went into a slow decline, he turned his talent to a number of writing and recording projects and was also gaining a reputation as an arranger and producer. Roger Christian: 'There wasn't anything beyond Gary's grasp. He could do anything from ghost songs, surf songs to hot rod songs to any kind of thing.'

One of the first projects he masterminded was *R.P.M.* coupled with *My Stingray* by The Four Speeds on the Challenge label. The Four Speeds were the start of many session groups he was to put together and featured Beach Boy Dennis Wilson on vocals and drums.

Released in July '63 the disc became a minor regional hit and was quickly followed by Gary Usher and The Usherettes *Three Surfer Boys* on the Dot label. The Usherettes were in fact The Honeys and it has been said that the vocal arrangements on the disc make it the most Honeys sounding of all the vocal sessions they did on other artist's records.

The song was written for Little Davy Summers (Russ Reagan) — the man who helped name The Beach Boys. However, he never got around to record it and so Gary decided to put it out himself and like Roger's debut disc it too failed to chart.

The disc's failure not to make the charts was just a little setback for Gary who had been busy putting together a session crew that in one form or another would work with Usher under several pseudonyms throughout the whole surf/hot rod era . . . starting out as The Super Stocks.

Gary Usher: 'The members of The Super Stocks were Churck Girard, Joe Kelly, Richie Podoler, Richard Burns, myself and any friend of mine who happened to be in the studio at the time I was cutting. Needless to say, the situation was very loose.' The Super Stocks' first recorded efforts were featured on the controversial Capitol *Shut Down* album . . . their songs, penned by Usher and Christian included *Wide Track, Four on the Floor, Street Machine* and *Cheater Slicks* and had an almost country feel to them.

*Street Machine* as *Little Street Machine* was later released by Roger Christian under the pseudonym Hot Rod Rog while *Cheater Slicks* coupled with *Four on the Floor* became The Four Speeds second outing.

Right from the outset Usher knew how to make a little go a long way. The Super Stocks went on to record three albums for Capitol, *Thunder Road, Surf Route 101* and *School Is A Drag.* (As a single he recorded *School Is A Drag* under the alias of The Wheelmen for Warner Brothers Records, albeit changing the title slightly by dropping *Drag* and inserting *Gas.*) The country feel of the early tracks gave way to a more contemporary West Coast sound and all the songs were arranged and conducted by Gary while the production credit went to in-house producer Jim Economides. The latter album featured such songs as *Readin'*,

*Ridin' and Racin'*, a song co-written by Sebastian Stores and a young Harry Nilsson, Usher and Christian's *No Wheels* and Usher's original title song.

Gary was also in great demand as a producer. Roger Christian: 'There were all different kinds of producers; Brian in the early days was more into vocals, Jan was into tracks and Gary was into both tracks and vocals.'

His first production credits included The Sunsets' *Chug-A-Lug*, *Lonely Surfer Boy* and *Surfin' Woodie* and Don Brandon's *Ballad of Bonneville*. While over at American Decca, in-house producer Charles Dant called in Gary and his crew, plus The Honeys to help finish The Surfaris second album *Hit City '64*.

Gary was still signed to Capitol at the time, so his production work on The Surfaris' *Sugar Shack*, *Be True To Your School* and *Wax, Board and Woodie* went uncredited.

*Wax, Board and Woodie* was another Usher/Christian original from the same writing sessions that produced The Astronauts' *Competition Coupe* and The Pyramids' *Midnight Run*.

Usher also produced The Surfaris' next single *Karen* and its flip side featured Usher and Christian's *Hod Rod High*.

The lead vocal was handled by Surfari Ron Wilson while the backing vocals featured Chuck Girard, Joe Kelly and Usher himself.

Gary was also becoming increasingly involved with the lucrative Beach movie industry supplying songs and even appearing in a couple including *Muscle Beach Party*, for example. Another of his cinema city assignments gave him the job of musical consultant to the Paramount movie *The Girls On The Beach*. Musically the film featured The Crickets, Lesley Gore and The Beach Boys.

The Beach Boys not only supplied the title song but the Wilson/Usher composition *The Lonely Sea* and a new Wilson/Love song *Little Honda*. Knowing The Beach Boys had no plans of releasing the latter song as a single, Usher (realizing the potential of the song) got his crew together, signed to Mercury and as The Hondells released *Little Honda* in September '64. It quickly rose into the top ten.

Along with his usual band of musical mercenaries Gary also brought in other friends to help out with The Hondells sound. Brian Wilson also co-wrote the second Hondells single *My Buddy Seat*.

Gary Usher: 'Bruce Johnston, Terry Melcher and Brian Wilson were on a lot of those early recordings. We were all friends and were continually (at the dismay of record companies) stopping in at each others sessions.'

Apart from helping Gary write the second Hondells hit, Brian was also present for the session that produced its flip-side ... *You're Gonna Ride With Me*. Chuck Girard: 'In fact we're both singing it together because he wanted to camouflage his voice a little.'

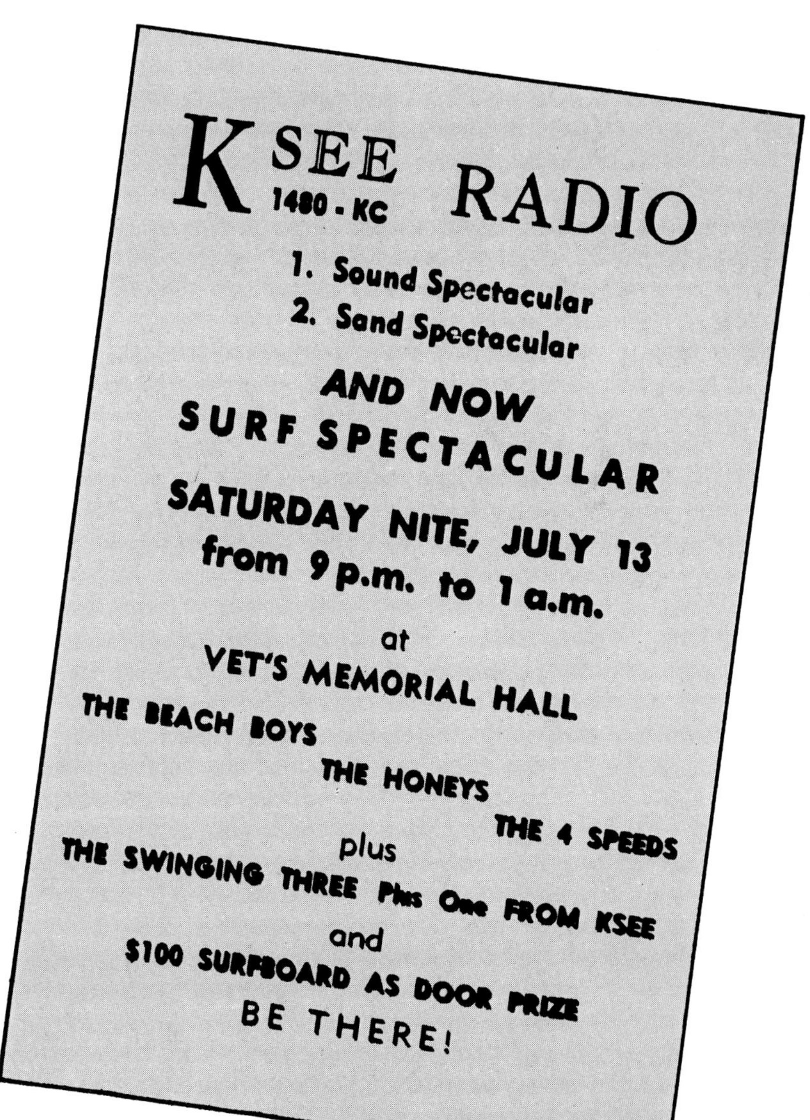

Along with a couple of albums The Hondells also went on to add music to the Honda advertising campaign 'You Meet The Nicest People on a Honda' and a commercial for Pepsi Cola.

With the success of their chart singles, Mercury Records insisted that there should be a performing Hondells. Girard: 'Dick Burns, who was one of the background singers, put the band together and then when the album came out (*Go Little Honda*), it said 'Featuring Richie Burns' because they wanted a band identification, because those guys behind him on those motorcycles on the first album cover are bank tellers, you see, Richie Burns was a manager of a bank. Those guys weren't even musicians — then they really got a group identity finally and started playing tours and got themselves together.'

The Hondell pretenders, not only performed live, but appeared in numerous teen movies. Roger Christian in '64: 'The Hondells are featured on the current cross-country Dick Clark tour. At the completion of the tour they head for Hollywood to shoot a new American International picture!' Under the musical guidance of Gary Usher, The Hondells appeared in *Ski Party* ('65), *Beach Blanket Bingo* ('65) and *Beach Ball* ('65). Chuck Girard: 'Ritchie Burns was the face to my voice. In fact, in the films The Hondells appeared in, it was my voice coming out of his mouth. That was kinda strange. We'd do all the music and they would do the actual filming.'

Their first album *Go Little Honda* not only featured Usher's regular session crew, but ole' dependable Glen Campbell playing guitar and singing the bass parts. The touring Hondells were becoming a big attraction helped by their many movie and TV appearances and were booked for the Australian Surfside '65 tour — the follow up of the highly successful Beach Boys/Surfaris outing the year before. Due to start in January, the tour was called off in late November '64 as the Australian promoters quickly realized surfin' wasn't as popular as the emerging UK scene, and changed the concept to The Big Beat Show, featuring The Rolling Stones. However, it wasn't all bad news for the outfit for they were now beginning to participate more and more on the recording side and one of the sessions produced the group's last big hit. Turning their attentions to folk rock, touring member Randy Thomas got to sing lead vocal on their cover of The Lovin' Spoonful's *Younger Girl*. Produced by Mike Curb and arranged by Usher the disc quickly rose into the top fifty, while its flip-side featured *All American Girl* co-written by Richard Burns and Gary.

Prior to the folk rock explosion Gary had been busy exploiting a new fad . . . slot-car racing. What skateboards were to surf-boards, slot-carts were to dragsters. Slot racing was a type of model scale-electric, in which two model dragsters (powered by batteries), ran down a model drag strip.

At a 'Teen Fair' held at Burbank, Tom Wolfe described for *Esquire* magazine his encounter with Dick Dale and slot-racing. Wolfe: 'Dick Dale, rigged out in Byronic shirt and blue cashmere V-neck sweater and wraparound sunglasses, singers mufti USA, has one cord with a start button, while

**Far left: The touring Hondells share one buddy seat.**

**Below: Ritchie Burns lip-syncs to the voice of Chuck Girard in *Ski Party* (1965).**

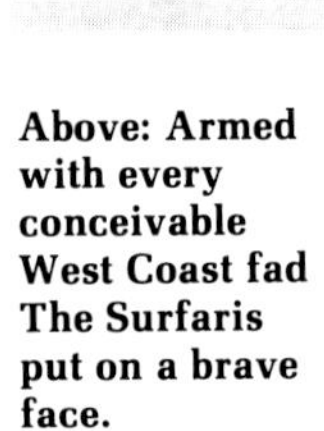

**Above: Armed with every conceivable West Coast fad The Surfaris put on a brave face.**

a bouffant nymphet from Newport named Sherma, Sherma of the Capri pants, has the other one. Don Beebe flashes a starting light and Sherma lets out a cry, not a thrilled cry, just nerves and a model 1963 Ford and a model dragster go running down the slot board, which is about chest high.'

The slot board was designed to be: one-twenty-fifth of the actual size of a drag strip. If you might be wondering the outcome of the Dick and Sherma contest, Wolfe never informed us.

Usher gathered his old reliables, tagged them The Revells (probably after the model-kit company) and produced the album *Go Sound Of The Slots* for Reprise Records. Around the same time as The Hondells success, Usher secured himself the job as full-time producer with American Decca and he turned his attentions to The Surfaris fulltime. The group were due to make a follow-up to their successful *Hit City '64* album. Now, with Gary firmly at the helm, things were to be different. . . . For Gary had decided that the main part of the group had already out-lived the usefulness. Usher: 'If you took Ron out of the group they were just a bunch of kids on stage playing three chords.'

Surfaris' leader and bass player Pat Connelly left in disgust; while the other members chose to turn a blind-eye. However, life became increasingly hard under the Usher regime, whereas before they were allowed at least too perform the instrumentals and especially their own originals, now Usher had other plans. For The Surfaris' *Hit City '65* album, Gary brought in his whole session crew. Using Ron Wilson as lead vocalist they covered a host of hits including The Beach Boys' *Dance, Dance, Dance* and Goffin and King's *I'm Into Something Good.*

Unfortunately, the rest of The Surfaris weren't included, they were left to record only four cuts . . . The Beatles' *She's A Woman*, The Everleys' *Gone, Gone, Gone*, Tommy Tucker's *Hi Heel Sneakers* (a live version) and The Detergents' *Leader of the Laundromat*. The latter, a send-up of The Shangri-Las *Leader Of The Pack* didn't appear on the UK release, it was substituted by a feeble cover-version of The Shadows' *The Rise And Fall of Flingel Bunt*. An instrumental The Surfaris themselves were unaware of recording, in fact the only other instrumental to feature on the US album was Burns and Podogers *Beat '65*, basically a re-working of Duane Eddy's *Movin' 'N' Groovin'*.

Usher and the crew, using Ron's lead vocal even covered (their) The Hondells' *My Buddy Seat*, and *Black Denim*.

*Black Denim*, a truly punk and underrated song came from the pen of Usher and Christian. Roger Christian also found more track to cover on the bike theme by collaborating with Mike Curb (later to be Governor of California) on The Buddies' *Little Iddy Biddy Buddy Rider* — a song best forgotten.

Usher in turn, plus crew became The Kickstands for a one-stand album *Black Boots and Bikes*, back on the old Capitol stomping ground.

Back on The Surfaris beat, where Gary was stating such nice things as 'I had no idea how talented the guys were as a group, or what their individual abilities were. But after we did these sides, their tremendous versatility and unique sound really impressed me. I think their biggest asset is their ability to achieve their recording identity quickly on a session.'

Was he really talking about the group, or his own band of reliables? However, he did allow the group to record their own instrumental *Battle Of The Iron Maiden*, albeit put-out as the flip-side of *Something Else* — their cover (only featuring Ron Wilson) of the Eddie Cochran favourite.

For his next Surfaris' single, Gary chose Brian Wilson's *Don't Hurt My Little Sister*, coupled with his own *Catch A Little Ride With Me*, the latter no doubt influenced by Brian's *Amusement Parks U.S.A.*), as with the forementioned single, it failed to make any impression on the charts.

Although the hits, were by now becoming few and far between, Capitol Records still had a huge appetite for West Coast trivial pursuits. And Gary, not one to let golden opportunities pass him by had plenty to offer . . . They included The Knights *Hot-Rod High*, The Ghouls *Dracula's Deuce*, plus his own (Brian Wilson produced) country

flavoured salute to the states capitol city . . . *Sacramento*.

On The Knight's album the crew were aided by Bob and Peter Klimes, apart from their authentic cover versions of The Beach Boys' *I Get Around* and *Be True To Your School*, Usher and Christian offered the title song while the Klimes co-authored the whimsical *Lonely Little Stocker*. *Be True To Your School* was revisited again, this time as *Be True To Your Ghoul*, along with *The Little Old Lady from (Pasadena) Transylvania* on The Ghoul's *Draculas Deuce* album.

If enough, wasn't enough . . . then Usher took it to the limit with The Silly Surfers album, orginally released as *The Sounds Of The Silly Surfers* as a promotional gimmick for the Hawk Model Company. The album produced by (if you believe it) Reuben Klamer, originally was distributed on the Hairy label until Mercury Records took-up the option and distributed the album nationally. It has now, as then, become a minor-sought after classic.

Unfortunately, the dawn was breaking on a new pop era, Usher and Christian had finally rode the final pure — Californian wave — from Beach Boys to Silly Surfers — they above all others, echoed the dreams of their generation. The youthful spirit and optimism of their time and place had never been captured in such the same way as the songs credited to Usher/Christian.

# Sidewalk Surfers: *The Ballad of Jan and Dean*

*It all started back in '63*
*With Jan and Dean, The Beach Boys and me*
*Hot Rod U.S.A.* — Terry Melcher/Bobby Darin

**Maybe the opening lyric should have included: It started back in '58 after Jan and Arnie and Dean became teammates! For the group had plenty of lead time and hits before the surf crowd caught up with them.**

Jan Berry (born 3 April 1941) and Dean Torrence (born 10 March 1940) both attended Emerson Jr. High School in West Los Angeles. However, they didn't become buddies until their final year at University High School when they started singing together. Their vocalizing really started in the school's echo-laden shower room after playing for the Varsity football team. Together with a couple of other team-mates they would plunder the repertoire of The Silhouettes, Danny and The Juniors and a host of other doo-wop outfits.

Unfortunately, their steamy singing sessions came to an abrupt end when the football season gave way to baseball. Not to be put off and completely hooked on making music, Jan and Dean went about forming a group . . . The Barons.

Dean Torrence: 'At the time we had six guys in the group: Chuck Steele was our lead singer because he was colored, Arnie Ginsberg was first tenor because he was Jewish, Wally Yagi was second tenor because he was a Jap, John Sagi Saligman was also second tenor because Wally didn't sing very loud. Jan Berry was the bass singer because he was the biggest and I sang all the high stuff because I was the only one that could.' With this multi-racial band of singers, two tape recorders and a microphone (borrowed from the school's auditorium) Jan set-up a recording studio in his parent's garage. This original garage band soon enlisted the help of musician friends and neighbours including Bruce Johnston on piano and Sandy Nelson on drums. Jan used two tape recorders, so that he could create a tape delay by going from one machine to the other in an attempt to simulate their shower-room echo affect.

Just as Jan was becoming adept at this ingenious recording technique most of the group members started to drop out for one reason or another.

Arnie Ginsberg, for one, couldn't make it to practice sessions because he was steady dating a girl he'd met down at the Frostee Freeze.

Jan and Dean pioneered on regardless, and penned their first song *Sally She Lived Upon The Hill* in the Spring of '58. One evening while rehearsing in Jan's garage, Arnie dropped by to tell them that he'd broken-up with his steady, and that he'd seen a girl he liked even better . . . a stripper by the name of Jennie Lee.

Ginsberg quickly talked the two impressionable youths into accompanying him down to the Follies Burlesk to catch her act. Dean: 'Upon sitting down (as far back as we could), the show started. Jennie came out dancing and even Jan said, "She had the two biggest 'you-know-whats' I have ever seen."'

Later that night while crusin' home in Jan's '57 Chevie the three Lee fans started up a doo-wop chant; Jan added a simple lyric line and the song *Jenny Lee* was born. Soon after, all three were in Jan's garage recording their new song.

Weeks later Dean left to join the army and it was left to Jan to try and place the tape. One of his first calls was at the office of Arwin Records, a minor LA label that was owned by Doris Day and Marty Melcher. Joe Lubin who ran the company, liked the song and purchased the raw tape, gave it to arranger Don Ralke to add some music and released it in April '58.

As Dean was away in the army the disc was credited to Jan and Arnie and it quickly entered the national top ten, selling around 850,000 copies. Jan and Arnie were soon back in the studio cutting their follow-up single *Gas Money*.

The song coupled with *Bonnie Lou* was released on Arwin Records in the following July and inched its way into the top hundred. Their third single *I Love Linda* was a complete flop, disenchanted Arnie quit (although he did later record *Women from Zanzibar* as The Rituals on Arwin).

Not long after Arnie's departure, Dean was demobbed and Jan asked him if he wanted to record again. He agreed, anything seemed better than taking a job at Dick Martin's Chevron — his only other offer. Shortly afterwards Dean received a call from Ginsberg who offered him his name 'for a percentage of the profits'. Torrence almost accepted. Dean: 'It's a good thing I didn't or I'd still be Arnie Ginsberg today!'

While Dean was away in the army, Jan struck up an acquaintance with Lou Adler that on Dean's return turned into a working relationship. Adler had been writing songs and arranging the discs with his partner Herb Alpert for Keen Records and found some success with Sam Cooke's *All In My Life* and *Wonderful World* among others.

Herb Alpert: 'We then started working with Jan and Dean, and I think it was at this point we left Keen Records. We felt we were at the end of a road there because the company had grown way beyond its capabilities.'

The first song Adler and Alpert suggested they should record was *Baby Talk*. Dean: 'We worked on *Baby Talk* for about two months. Yes, you might say two months seems like a long time to work on a song, especially when it was only two minutes and 17 seconds long. But, as I remember, we would sing (learn) about 4 bars at a time (which wasn't that unheard of) but between those bars we would go to the beach or down the street and visit some girls or maybe even cruise Goody-Goody's, a popular local drive-in.

'Once we finished putting on our voices and piano, Lou Adler had his friend, Herb Alpert, write the arrangements. Then, we went into the studio and combined the rhythm section with our vocal tape — that's all there was to it.'

*Baby Talk* coupled with *Jeanette Get Your Hair Done* was finally placed with Dore Records. The company had recently had a huge hit with another LA based outfit, The Teddy Bears and *To Know Him Is To Love Him*. They weren't disappointed when Jan and Dean's disc charted in September '59 reaching the number ten slot, nationally.

It was also a great shot-in-the-arm for Jan, Dean, Lou and Herb, albeit, the first few hundred copies were released under the Jan and Arnie credit. Due to the enormous popularity of the disc Jan and Dean made their debut on Dick Clark's nationally networked TV show *American Bandstand*.

A string of Dore singles followed including *There's A Girl* (their first written by Adler and Alpert), *Clementine* and *White Tennis Sneakers*. *Clementine* was the first Berry/Torence collaboration, that unfortunately was released at the same time as Bobby Darin's version of this traditional standard. Jan and Dean were amazed to find that their version hit the charts at

**Below and opposite: The all-American clean-cut image of the early Jan and Dean.**

number 40, just six days after it had been available in the shops. The following week Billboard's error was corrected and Bobby Darin's name was added to the hit and theirs dropped . . . Jan and Dean's *Clementine* finally peaked at number 65.

For their next chart assault the duo covered The Moonglows' *We Go Together*, which crept into the top fifty, quickly followed by *Gee* — the first song they ever recorded outside of Jan's garage — at Western no less, albeit on a two track machine.

In 1961, they also appeared as part of the line-up for the (Herb B. Lou Productions) Dante and The Evergreens cover version of The Hollywood Argyles' *Alley-Op*. Released on Madison Records it charged up the charts capturing the number 15 slot, leaving the original to claim number one.

Another top twenty smash for the team and several thousand dollars to claim in royalties. Unfortunately they never received a cent. Alpert: 'The Government moved in and closed Madison Records. The Internal Revenue was first in line, and then a couple of other people, so to collect our money through the courts we had absolutely no chance.'

Back at Dore Records, a couple more singles were released plus an album without any great deal of success . . . it was time to move on, and move on they did. Jan and Dean cut *Heart and Soul* independently. Looking back, Dean recalled that Herb Alpert didn't like *Heart and Soul* and insisted that they should place 'some trumpet song he had recorded' instead. Outvoted by Lou, Jan and Dean and feeling disenchanted by the industry, Herb took off to enroll in acting classes (before returning to the record business, forming A&M Records and The Tijuana Brass).

Lou carried on as Jan and Dean's full-time manager. His first objective was to place the duo with a major label. So, armed with the *Heart and Soul* demo, he approached Liberty Records. Knowing their track record, Liberty were impressed by the singers but, less than enthusiastic about their choice of material. After all, who in '61 would contemplate any chart mileage in an old Hoagy Carmichael classic?

Not one to be put off that easily, Adler soon placed the disc with Challenge

Records and it catapulted into the top thirty . . . weeks later, Jan and Dean were signed to Liberty. (Although the group had to fulfil a two record deal with Challenge and rushed out *Wanted One Girl* in August '61. It quickly sank into obscurity.)

For their first Liberty outing, the duo chose *A Sunday Kind of Love*, but again it failed to make any great impression on the charts. Fearing the worst, Liberty handed them over to their top in-house producer Snuff Garrett (a name probably more synonymous with the string of MOR *50 Guitar* albums) to hopefully come up with the goods. The resulting platter, *Tennesee*, only did fractionally better than their Liberty debut. To help recoup their investment, Liberty obtained the rights to the earlier Jan and Dean and Arnie hits and repackaged them as *Jan and Dean's Golden Hits*. As the tracks available didn't quite make an albums worth, the duo were asked for some (cheaply produced) extra material.

Dean: 'Since we hadn't made much money for Liberty, they wouldn't give us much of a budget to work with. This meant we would have to do all the background vocals ourselves. One of the relics we did for this album was *Barbara Ann* (originally done by The Regents). Jan and I sang all the background parts and I sang the lead, all in falsetto-high voice stuff. Once we finished and listened, we liked what we heard, a new sound kinda. We then looked for another song, preferably about a girl that lent itself to a falsetto lead and some good vocal background parts. *Linda* had what we were looking for. We cut it and it made it.'

*Linda* rose quickly into the top thirty, although the song had already seen some popularity via Buddy Clark. In fact, *Linda* was written by Jack Lawrence, at the suggestion of his accountant Lee Eastman (to write a song about his daughter . . . The Lovely Linda).

Jan and Dean injected a more contemporary feel into their version, reminiscent of the sound of the East Coast, Four Seasons and close to home, The Beach Boys. Dean: 'Surfing music had just arrived and Jan and I were physically involved in surfing, so it was just natural that we became involved with the music.'

Around this time, Jan and Dean appeared on a show with The Beach Boys. Dean: 'When *Surfin'* came out, we heard it and liked it. We weren't afraid of it at all, in fact I think we sensed that it was going to help, that it would be good for business — it would be good to have more California groups, because we didn't have that many out here. But I think what really did it was a concert that we did with them right after *Surfin'*. I think they'd recorded *Surfin' Safari*, and it had just been out a couple of weeks, and had got a lot of plays, so we were familiar with it. We did this concert together, and they were to back us, so we met in a house trailer, where we changed, plus we sat around and taught them our repertoire of four songs. They came out and did their songs and a couple of instrumentals, and then we came out and did our three or four songs — I don't think we had many that we could do live! When we'd done our set, the crowd were really excited, an excitement that we'd never really felt before, because it was a male audience as well as a female audience for the first time. Really nice, a bigger mass of people out there. So after we finished our three songs, which had nothing particularly to do with surfing, we realized that they wanted more, so we asked The Beach Boys, "Hey do you want to do your set again, and we'll sing with you guys?"; because we all knew the parts, easy parts, and in fact we could do some of the parts they couldn't do. So they said "Gee, you'll sing our songs?", and I said "sure, I think your songs are really fun to sing." So we sang *Surfin'* and *Surfin' Safari*, and really had a ball singing them. And we really listened to those parts that Brian was writing, they sounded simple but they were really great. I remember driving home after that, and saying "Man, those parts are really good, they're really fun to sing. Maybe we should give Brian a call next week and see if he's got any tunes!" So we had *Linda*, yet we wanted to do surfing and somebody, probably Lou Adler said "Why don't you take Linda surfing, and do an album called *Jan and Dean Take Linda Surfing*. That gets it all in there.' So we agreed to that, except that we didn't know any surfing songs except the two that The Beach Boys had done.

'So we called up Brian and said "Brian, we've got a hit record with *Linda*, we're going to do an album with a fairly good budget, but we need your help. Would you come on in and play the tracks for us to *Surfin'* and *Surfin' Safari*, and we'll put them on our album?"

'He was just totally knocked out that we were going to record his songs! He said "Sure I'll get the guys", and all of them showed up at the studio, and we got reintroduced to one another, and sat around drinking beer and stuff and they played the two tracks, sang all the background parts with us.

'We sang essentially what we sang on stage that one night. Then Brian showed us stuff he'd been doing, like dualing voices and even dualing background vocals. We were used to dualing leads and maybe falsettos, but never the four parts, and he showed us how to do the four parts over again. And that was it, that was really the key to the whole thing.'

Also, while at the session, Brian gave them a sneak-preview of The Beach Boys forthcoming single . . . *Surfin' U.S.A.* Jan loved the song and asked Brian if there was any chance of Jan and Dean putting it out. Brian refused, but offered the duo two other compositions: *(When Summer Comes) Gonna Hustle You* and another he hadn't fully completed. However, the opening line 'Two Girls For Every Boy' was enough for Jan to say 'We'll take it!'. Brian had also worked out the melody line, so it was left to Jan to complete the lyrics. Roger Christian: 'Jan liked the song *Shut Down* (the flip-side of *Surfin' U.S.A.*) and he asked me to write a song with him called *Surfin' Woodie* and he changed it around and called it *Surf City* and wrote it with Brian.'

*I bought a thirty four wagon and we called it a woodie Surf City, here we come*

Both Murry Wilson and Capitol Records became annoyed when they learnt that Brian had even appeared on the disc.

Christian: 'Mr Wilson thought that Jan was always picking Brian's brain. Brian would always sing on the Jan and Dean songs mixed in with a little bit of Dean and this aggravated Mr Wilson.'

*Surf City* became Jan and Dean's first number one hit single and catapulted them to the forefront of surf music. The disc also marked the first time Jan Berry was credited as arranger and producer.

The album *Jan and Dean Take Linda Surfin'* (May '63) was also released in the same month confirming their newly acquired status. Hot on its heels followed *Surf City and Other Swingin' Cities* — an album rushed out to capitalize on the singles success. Although it featured little in the way of surf music (including as it did such diverse tracks as *Way Down Yonder In New Orleans* and *I Left My Heart In San Francisco*), it did feature, however, the duo's follow-up single *Honolulu Lulu*, plus some great session players such as Hal Blaine and Glen Campbell.

As the summer of '63 faded, Jan, once again called in Brian Wilson and Roger Christian to help out on their latest single, *Drag City*. It too quickly varoomed its way up the charts and into the Jan and Dean legend.

An album of the same name was also released, establishing them with the auto-crowd and giving Roger Christian another opportunity to accelerate his writing skill. They simply scorched off his pad! *I Gotta Drive*, *Surf Route 101* and *Dead Man's Curve* to name a few. While the album also fea-

Never Before So Many Stars!
Never Before Such Value!

MURRAY the K's
HOLIDAY REVUE
AT THE
BROOKLYN FOX THEATRE
ON FLATBUSH AVE. in BROOKLYN, N. Y.
10 Big Days - Aug. 30 thru Sept. 8
Continuous Performances — Morning Till Night

STARRING
BEN E. KING
"STAND BY ME" • "I" (WHO HAVE NOTHING)
LITTLE STEVIE WONDER
"FINGERTIPS"
JAN AND DEAN
"LINDA" • "SURF CITY"
THE DRIFTERS
"ON BROADWAY" • "UP ON THE ROOF"
THE SHIRELLES
"WILL YOU LOVE ME TOMORROW"
"DON'T SAY GOODNIGHT AND MEAN GOODBYE"
GENE PITNEY
"TOWN WITHOUT PITY"
"TRUE LOVE NEVER RUNS SMOOTH"
THE MIRACLES
"MICKEY'S MONKEY"
"YOU'VE REALLY GOT A HOLD ON ME"
PAUL & PAULA
"HEY PAULA" • "FIRST QUARREL"
THE ANGELS
"TIL" • "MY BOY FRIEND'S BACK"
THE DOVELLS
"BRISTOL STOMP" • "YOU CAN'T SIT DOWN"
JAY AND THE AMERICANS
"SHE CRIED" • "ONLY IN AMERICA"
THE TYMES
"SO MUCH IN LOVE" • "WONDERFUL, WONDERFUL"
THE CHIFFONS
"HE'S SO FINE" • "ONE FINE DAY"
RANDY AND THE RAINBOWS
"DENISE"



tured a J and D cover of *Little Deuce Coupe* with a lead vocal handled by Mike Love and some great guitar lines care of Glen Campbell.

However, Beach Boys Brian and Mike weren't alone in their moonlighting activities. Now a producer in his own right, Jan began working part-time for the Colpix label. The Madators' *Perfidia* was to become his first production venture outside of Jan and Dean Product. Albeit, The Matadors were their backing group, and for his second — The Matadors' *I Gotta Drive* (a song taken from the *Drag City* album), he even employed himself, his girlfriend Jill Gibson and Dean to become basically a Jan and Dean disc. Dean: 'We just had too many tracks for single release under our own name.' Unfortunately, both discs joined the ranks of rock trivia. He fared little better with *He Don't Love Me*, recorded by another one-time girlfriend Shelly Fabares.

For the record; Jill Gibson had been Jan's most consistent date since the summer of 1960. She had also contributed on a number of songs with Jan and long-time friend Don Altfeld. Starlette Shelly Fabares later became Mrs Lou Adler.

Thankfully, Jan and Dean's discs continued to break big. Their next single became a double-sided hit coupling a remixed *Dead Man's Curve* with *A New Girl in School*, the latter reaching the top forty, while its flip-side made number eight in the National hot hundred. Dean Torrence once recalled the story behind *The New Girl In School*: 'This song was originally titled, *When Summer Comes, Gonna Hustle You*, which was written by Brian Wilson and was given to us at the same session he gave us *Surf City*. We recorded it before *Surf City* but when we played it for people, adult type, they would exclaim: "You can't say 'hustle you' on the radio" . . . well, we didn't know what the hell they were talking about, so rather than argue, we finished *Surf City* and rewrote *Gonna Hustle You* so that it became *The New Girl In School*.'

The song was finally credited to Brian Wilson, Jan Berry, Roger Christian and Bob Norman.

Their next single *Little Old Lady From Pasadena*, did even better, reaching the number three spot and was quickly followed by a lawsuit. Roger Christian: 'Yes we all got sued on that, Jan, Jill, Don etc. The lawsuit was dropped when the song became a Screen Gems song rather than a Trousdale Music song.'

Trousdale Music was a company owned by Lou Adler, at the same time as forming Trousdale, Adler had also formed Dunhill Productions and signed on a young song-writing team by the name of Steve Barri and Phil Sloan. Part of the songsmiths brief was to supply material for Jan and Dean who were both (at the time) attending courses at the University of Southern California and could not fulfil their Liberty commitment for new material . . . which was growing by the day.

For example, Liberty rushed out an album based on their double-sided hit *Dead Man's Curve/The New Girl In School* and included among its programme *Linda* . . . a long ago triumph! Apart from the Berry, Christian: *Three Window Coupe*, the album only offered one hot-rod classic: *Bucket "T"* (later covered by Ronny and The Daytonas and The Who). What with their Liberty obligations and their individual studies, the relationship between Jan and Dean became strained. Phil Sloan: 'At one point Jan wanted me to be Jan and Dean. I was doing background parts, doubling Jan's lead on a *Little Old Lady From Pasadena*, I did the falsetto. Dean wasn't there at all. He was having another feud with Jan.'

Aside from their in-fighting and feuds, Lou Adler had bigger plans for his boys. He wanted them on celluloid . . . to become movie stars. His first plan was to have them appear with Shelly Fabares in Columbia Pictures' *Ride The Wild Surf*. Unfortunately, his plan never materialized, and only Shelly ended-up starring in the film. Jan and Dean were eventually replaced by Peter Brown and Tab Hunter, nevertheless they still got the title song. *Ride The Wild Surf*, again co-written by Berry, Wilson and Christian wiped-out the top twenty while the album of the same name was graced by a sleeve note by Shelley Fabares: 'There have been many quotes, sayings, etc to depict a good time, such as "More fun than a barrel of monkeys, You're a barrel of laughs" etc'. She wrote, 'Anyone who had been around Jan and Dean will not be too surprised if in the not-so-distant future someone says "You're more fun than a barrel of Jan and Deans", because anyone who has been fortunate enough to come in contact with these two slapstick kids from California knows that nothing could be more fun than Jan and Dean, except a barrel of them. Their quick humour and Laurel and Hardy antics have literally broken up disc-jockeys and audiences from New York to the surf at Waimea Bay.'

**Above: Kissing their rights away with *The Little Old Lady From Pasadena*.**

This Laurel and Hardy/clown princes of surfdom tag, went some way in insuring them the engagement as MC's in a forthcoming international pop spectacular . . . *The T.A.M.I. Show*, to be held on 24/10/64 at the Santa Monica Civic Auditorium.

*The Ride The Wild Surf* album surfaced in August '64 and hot on its heels followed *The Little Old Lady From Pasadena*. Apart from featuring an ever increasing input of songs from Sloan and Barri, including such cult favourites as *Tell 'Em I'm Surfin'*, *Summer Means Funs* and *One-Piece Topless Bathing Suit*, both albums featured tunes built around the latest Californian fad skate-boarding.

The strongest track *Sidewalk Surfin'*

quickly rose into the top thirty. When released as a single. Dean Torrence: 'Well, we had noticed that a lot of kids were riding skateboards around California and we thought, "Gee that would be a good idea for a song", and I think we attempted to sit down and write something but we couldn't come up with anything that we were happy with, and in recalling The Beach Boys song *Catch A Wave*, I thought "Boy, that's a really beautiful melody" and with Brian's permission (I think he even helped write some of the new words) we just really changed the lyrics. That was a lot of fun. It gave kids an opportunity to really feel like they were surfing, outside of surfing areas. It was something that a whole lot more people at this point could relate to directly more than surfing.'

There was even a story behind the discs atmospheric opening. Torrence: 'To get a recording of a skateboard we put a long cord on a microphone so we could record out in front of the recording studio on the sidewalk. Jan said he was better at crashing. So we recorded him doing his famous wipe-out act and thats how the record starts.' Jan and Dean's other adventures into the genre consisted of two instrumentals (both penned by Jan and Jill Gibson), *Skate-boarding Part I* and *Part II*.

Plus a little merchandizing operation on the side that took the form of Jan and Dean's Little Old Lady Skateboards.

They even opened that *T.A.M.I. Show* armed with skateboards. The show itself featured a pot pourrie of rock styles from The Beach Boys to Marvin Gaye to Chuck Berry and Lesley Gore. The concert was filmed by Steve Binder and finally released under an assortment of titles . . . *The Tami Show* ('65) *Gather No Moss* or *Teenage Command Performance* . . . It was the same show, whatever the title.

Over the opening credits (of the various titles), Jan and Dean performed Sloan and Barri's *From All Over The World* — a song famous for introducing The Rolling Stones as coming from Liverpool. Accurate or not, the disc climbed safely into the top fifty. Liberty quickly rushed out the *Command Performance — Live In Person* album, designed to cash in on the rock extravaganza. Unfortunately, the recording wasn't from the *Tami Show* but from live recordings of the group's many appearances at Sacramento's Memorial Auditorium.

Behind the hits, life seemed to be becoming more difficult for the duo. Jan (as always) had his own way, when deciding what the duo would or wouldn't record. Dean: 'One of them, *You Really Know How to Hurt A Guy*, I hated so much that I refused to sing on it. The day the vocals were being put on it Jan told me to get the hell out of the studio while he was singing if I thought the song was so bad.'

Roger Christian: 'Dean didn't have any talent (musically) really. He had a falsetto voice but it wasn't a pure falsetto like Brian's. It could have been Jan and anybody.' With or without Dean, and at the height of the English invasion, the single reached number twenty-two in the National Charts. Jan decided to take some time out and worked closely with arranger/conductor George Tipton, Dean was eventually brought in and an album of Jan and Dean's hits classically arranged was released under the title *Jan and Dean's Pop Hit Symphoney No. 1.*

After the disappointment of their planned movie debut, Lou Adler was even more determined to get them on celluloid. The opportunity eventually arrived via the Paramount Pictures/Dunhill Productions *Easy Come, Easy Go.*

The movie (not to be confused with the Elvis Presley vehicle of the same name) was also to mark the big screen directional debut of comedy scriptwriter Mel Brooks. Shooting on the picture had only just got under way, when production was halted, after a runaway railroad car injured seventeen members of the cast and crew, Jan received a fractured leg in the incident. Evidence of his injuries (crutch and caste) can be seen on the front sleeve of their *Filet of Soul* album. The disc subtitled *A Live One* was in fact a compilation of left over live and studio out-takes. Apart from including a number of Beatle songs and chart hits of the day, the most interesting item was the original version of *The New Girl in School . . . (When Summer Comes) Gonna Hustle You.*

September '65 found the duo with another hit-parade smash; Sloan and Barris' *I Found A Girl.* While deep down in Jan's Bel Air studio the group began work on their 'BATTACULAR' album — *Jan and Dean Meet Batman.*

Released in March '66, the album's programme featured a storyline that was pure locker-room humour — introducing such soppy heroes as Capt Jan and Dean (the boy blunder). Just to break-up the (laugh, I wish I could have cried) humour lay six musical items . . . and, the best was the original Neal Heffi *Batman Theme* . . . thanks to Hal Blaine's tight drumming and arrangements.

Out of the three new Berry, Gibson and Altfeld compositions included on the album only *The Joker Is Wild* stood out; if only for its sheer banality. Although Liberty saw it fit to release their *Batman* as a single only (probably) for the lack of new Jan and Dean material.

To be fair to the project, it at least gave George Tipton (who helped out on the arrangements) a trial-run before Harry Nilsson's successful *The Point* Album. And, of course, it eventually turned out to be one of those albums you love to have on your shelf. But never play.

Not long after completing the album, Jill Gibson ended her long-lasting engagement, after catching Jan in a compromising position with two young female hitch-hikers.

Liberty in search of Jan and Dean hit

**Left: A scene from the ill-fated movie *Easy Come, Easy Go* . . . above: evidence of its downfall.**

material released *Norwegian Wood*, coupled with *Popsicle*. *Popsicle* had originally been released on the '63 *Drag City* Album, under the title *Popsicle Truck*.

The duo became incensed by the company's decision to release (as a major single) such a pedestrian version of the famous Beatle song. Dean: 'I had no control over what they put out. They just kept re-issuing stuff. Then they decided to put out *Norwegian Wood*, which was ludicrous. Our version didn't come close to The Beatle's version, and everyone owned The Beatle's version already, I told them not to, but they did anyway!' However, disc jockey's started playing the flip-side ... and *Popsicle* became Jan and Dean's last top thirty hit single.

Just days after *Popsicle* was released Jan was due for an appointment before the draft board, as he approached the curve on Whittier Boulevard just below Sunset Boulevard the Corvette he was driving went out of control and hit a parked truck. Mike Barry (son of actor Gene Barry) was the first on the scene of the accident. Barry: 'Man, I heard this screech ... an incredibly long screech. I told someone in the house to call an ambulance and then went outside. By then the car had stopped. It was rammed into the rear of a parked truck. I mean the entire car was shattered. It was scattered over thc street in little chips. Only the steel frame was left. On the street were these long skid marks. He had to be doing 60 or 70 miles per hour.

'I ran up to the car. It was a Corvette. Either it had been a convertible or the top had been ripped off. He was in the driver's seat. At first he moved; I thought he was conscious. Then he slumped back. My first instinct was to get him out but the frame of

# 3 More Die In Traffic; Singer Hurt

LOS ANGELES Pop singer suffered critical injuries in the crash of his sports car which went out of control and struck a truck in Beverly Hills Tuesday.

Rescue squad officers inspect the wreckage.

— Three persons are dead and Jan Berry, singer, 25, a part of the team of Jan and Dean, is in serious condition at UCLA Medical Center as the result of traffic accidents during the last 24 hours, police reported today.

Berry, in a semi-conscious condition, was injured when he apparently lost control of his sports car and crashed into a parked truck. Several months ago he suffered a fractured leg when he fell from a railroad car while shooting a movie.

the door wouldn't open. I leaned in and then I saw his head. It was split open. A woman arrived and she was screaming. "Get him out! We gotta get him out!" I didn't see any reason to expect any kind of explosion or anything but what I did see was the gash — it went from his nose, past his forehead and into his hairline.

'No way, lady,' I said. 'We move him and we're going to kill him.'

The ambulance arrived and rushed Jan to UCLA Medical Center where his condition was said to be serious.

Dean later reported that: 'He suffered some brain damage and to this day is going to both physical and speech therapy classes and is constantly improving.'

Jan's unfortunate accident coincided with the fulfilment of their Liberty contract. So, with Dean now firmly at the helm, he went about business. The first thing he decided to do, was to set up his own record company, J&D Records. Dean: 'My main ambition was to learn about the record business from the inception of the recording all the way to distribution and sales. I wanted to learn production, and also I guess gamble a bit. It was also a ploy on my part to keep the Jan and Dean name alive.'

Liberty were also keen to keep the Jan and Dean name alive, and issued *Fiddle Around* (an, until then, unreleased track) which crept silently into the top hundred. J&D records, first release *Hawaii* coupled with *Tijuana*, was even less fortunate and disappeared without trace. Dean, continued by producing *Summertime, Summertime* again without any major chart action. Then he put out one of Jan's pre-accident, production numbers . . . *Louisiana Man*, it too sailed down the tubes.

Not to be put-off by his lack of chart success, Dean went about putting together an album that finally materialized as *Save For A Rainy Day*; released in March '67 the album took its title from the standard of the same name. Dean then went in search of a major distributor. Columbia Records decided to take a one-year option on Jan and Dean material, starting with the release of the *Yellow Balloon* single. . . . Columbia was also ready to distribute the *Rainy Day* album . . . but there was one problem, Jan wouldn't sign the contract, in fact he disliked the whole project and told Dean, 'I do

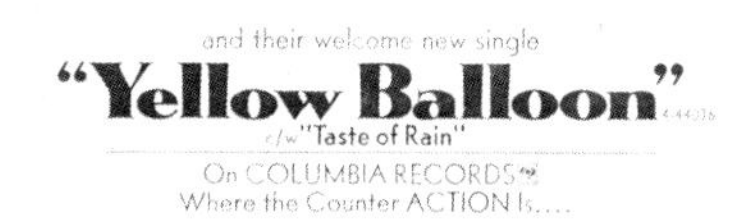


**Above: The Jan pictured is, in fact, his brother Bruce.**



it from now.'

Still determined to be Jan and Dean, Jan once again called upon the songwriting talent of Roger Christian.

Christian: 'Jan and I worked on some songs around that time — *I Can See Clearly, I Can See Forever, Rollercoasters On Rainbows* a lot of things we didn't finish. This was just after the accident, just out of the hospital — That was just his whole life, making records and he wanted to keep doing it, like he's still doing it now. Lou Adler made a contribution to him, gave him the studio time.'

And so, with a handful of new songs and a running feud with Dean, Jan went in search of a deal . . . and quickly found one at Warner Bros. Dean: 'I could have blown his deal; just like he blew mine with Columbia, but I decided not to, so he went along and recorded some stuff for Warners, but I wasn't involved in any of it. I might have sang on one of them, but that was about the total extent of my work. I did, in the beginning, go round with Jan to radio stations and try to peddle records; but actually the whole situation basically pissed me off. I didn't ask for any money, but he could have paid me the standard session fee, even if I wasn't there, for the use of our name and other help.'

Starting with *Only A Boy* in November '67 Jan released three singles on the Warner Brothers label (the best of which was probably Berry and Christian's *I Know My Mind* coupled with *Laurel & Hardy* — the latter being a complete version of *Roller-coasters On Rainbows*). Switching to Ode, he released another two singles, the first of which was accompanied by a press release that read: 'Hello out there, You know that Jan and Dean haven't done anything in a long time. But I've been recovering and have made my first record which is a ballad. Play it and see if you like it.'



Sadly, not many did and the Ode singles went in the same direction as the Warner Brothers ... nowhere. Dean, at the time, was having better luck first with his own graphic design company — Kittyhawk, turning out album sleeves for Harry Nilsson and others and then The Legendary Masked Surfers.

While working at UA Records on their *Legendary Masters* series, Dean came up with the idea of the Masked Surfers. He quickly called in his mates, Bruce Johnston and Terry Melcher and re-mixed and updated *Summertime, Summertime* and *Gonna Hustle You*. Dean: 'I'd say they were about ¾ths 90% cut; but we added some piano, percussion and vocals, then remixed the whole thing.'

Released at the height of the seventies surf-revival, the timing couldn't have been better and it was quickly followed by a new Jan and Dean double album compilation ... *Gotta Take That One Last Ride*. Torrence, Melcher and Johnston put out a second Masked Surfer's single: *Summer Means Fun* and then decided to form a new group ... California. Dean: 'We recorded two originals which could best be described as surf/reggae tunes. They were good, but the recording session didn't go as easy as some might have expected. I think Bruce and Terry expected too much the first time around; they thought we'd come on like instant Beatles or something ... Bruce was also afraid of being pigeonholed into being labelled a surfer again ... which he has been trying to get away from for years.' Plus; 'The record companies just never came up with the right deal.'

With the new-found interest in Jan and Dean's music the duo decided in '73 to get together. On their first outing they played a surf revival concert at the Hollywood Palladium, along with Dick Dale, The Surfaris and others. Billed as The Legendary Masked Surfers, they could only lip-synch their way through their big hits (owing to Jan's still unstable condition) ... but, at least they were on the road again.

One of the tracks that appeared on the *Gotta Take That One Last Ride* album, *Sunshine Music* found Dean accompanied by a new surf group Papa Doo Run Run and he also often appeared with them on stage at this time. In fact, he was instumental in getting the group their own record deal, by introducing them to Bruce Johnston. Johnston: 'There's absolutely nothing wrong with good, heavy metal records ... but lots of kids who I met at the concert for Papa Doo Run Run were saying why didn't we give them a record they could really identify with ... a good teen record' ... he soon found it for them with Papa Doo Run Run's powerful revival of The Beach Boys', *Be True To Your School*.

Jan and Dean's Hollywood Palladium concert became the climax of their bio-pic Deadman's Curve (1978). The movie starred Richard Hatch and Bruce Davidson with cameo appearances by Mike Love and Bruce Johnston.

Since the movie Jan has continued to improve and the duo have made numerous live appearances and in 1985 released a brand new album celebrating twenty seven years in the recording industry.

# Don't Back Down: *The Beach Boys Part II*

*I'm gettin' bugged, drivin' up an' down the same ol' strip*
*I gotta find a new place where the kids are hip*

*I Get Around* — Brian Wilson

**With *I Want to Hold Your Hand* topping the US single's charts and their first album rising fast, The Beatles hit America in February '64 — on a wave of publicity that was to swamp the world as the Liverpool Sound . . . It was also to be The Beach Boys' biggest challenge.**

In the same month as the mop-tops were captivating the American airwaves, the Beach boys released *Fun, Fun, Fun.* Mike Love: 'We were going from the Holiday Inn in Salt Lake City to the airport . . . I got the idea to do a song about a girl who borrows the car from her father and instead of going to the library like she tells him, goes cruisin' to see and be seen by all the boys. Her father finds out she didn't go to the library; she went to the hamburger stand. Yet when he takes the car keys away, the guy says, "Well, that's okay because now we'll have fun, fun, fun now that daddy took the T-Bird away." '

For the song's intro Brian re-worked Chuck Berry's *Johnny B. Goode* rhiff, to great affect and the whole song just motored along at a solid pace. Phil Spector: 'I remember when *Fun, Fun, Fun* came out. He (Brian) wasn't interested in the money, but wanted a top-ten record. He wanted to

know how the song would do against the Beatles and if KFWB would play it.'

The disc became their highest chart placing to date reaching number five in the national charts, and hot on its heels followed the album *Shut Down Vol. II*. *Shut Down Vol. II* also found The Beach Boys at full-steam . . . Brian's production expertise had flowered into almost Spectorian terms! Just one listen and you can almost hear the master's chains being dragged across the studio floor, on their rendition of the old Frankie Lymon hit *Why Do Fools Fall In Love*.

**Far right: The Beach Boys accompany Annette at the opening of *The Monkey's Uncle* (1965). The disc was released without credit to The Beach Boys.**

Then among the great selection of ballads (including *The Warmth Of The Sun*) we were offered the unbeatable *Don't Worry Baby*.

Add to that Dennis Wilson's rasping lead vocal on *This Car of Mine*, their hit single *Fun, Fun, Fun* and a couple of typical surf instrumentals — *Shut Down Part Two* and *Denny's Drums*, plus the all-time sixties group favourite *Louie, Louie* and record buyers surely realized, after exploring all the Californian fads, The Beach Boys had become one themselves.



Yet, they still had a long road ahead. Roger Christian: 'Capitol was throwing a big reception at the Beverly Wiltshire Hotel for Kyu Sakamoto, who had a big record called *Sukiyaki*. The Beach Boys had had a couple of big records for Capitol, but they didn't have a party. So I was going and I asked Brian to come with me . . . we were writing together. We got there, and Brian was talking to somebody and he came over kind of discouraged. Voyle Gilmore had told him that he had no business being there, he was upstaging Kyu. And I said, "Just a minute, you're here as my guest, and we're writing some songs that are eventually going to make this goddam company some money," one example of the typical things Capitol would do.'

Capitol Records, were at the time also distributing Beatles' product and just when the US singles charts were dominated by The Fabs, The Beach Boys stole the crown for the first time and reached the coverted number one slot with Brian's finest yet . . . *I Get Around*.

Then, while The Beatles were hard at work on their debut movie, The Beach Boys were also making headway on celluloid. In their first screen appearance they acted as back-up band for the queen on the beach bunnies; Annette Funicello in Walt Disney's *The Monkey's Uncle* (1965). Annette: 'They weren't as big then as they were soon to become. We did the song together for *The Monkey's Uncle* . . . The boys were very easy to work with. I was completely overwhelmed by Dennis, the drummer — He was so adorable and you could tell even then he was a real killer diller. His eyes were full of fire, and he was precocious, and everybody's favorite on the set. And all the others were just the nicest to work with,' (Brian appeared as an extra on a couple of other movies (one of his biggest roles was that of a beachnik in the company of Usher and Christian in *Muscle Beach Party* (1964)) 'but I never saw them again after *The Monkey's Uncle*.'

The Beach Boys' biggest screen appearance was (as themselves) in *The Girls On The Beach* (1965). They performed three songs in the film *The Lonely Sea*, *Little Honda* and the title song. Although there wasn't a soundtrack album made available, the latter songs were featured on their *All Summer Long* album.

Released in August '64, *All Summer Long*, above all their previous albums, captured the spirit of their special Californian lifestyle. Practically every element of West Coast teenage life was explored from *The Girls On The Beach*, *Drive In*, and *Little Honda* to *I Get Around*, *Wendy*, and *Don't Back Down*. *Don't Back Down* was also to mark their departure from the surf scene:

*With their feet full of tar and their hair full of sand*
*The boys know the surf like the back of their hands*

The song seemed to imply it was time to move on. Brian: 'People ask me sometimes how I come up with my ideas. Sometimes I don't know. The feelings you get from going to school, being in love, winning and losing in sports — these are my inspirations. A sociologist might say I am trying to generate a feeling of social superiority. I live with my piano and love to make records that my friends like to hear — My ideas for the group are to combine music that strikes deep emotional response among listeners and still maintains a somewhat untrained

and teenage sound.'

With the continued pressure from the English invasion, Brian was asking more and more from the group. Carl: 'I remember when we did *Little Honda*. Brian wanted to get this real distorted guitar sound, real fuzzy. "This guitar sounds like shit," I said and he goes, "Just do it." When I heard it, I felt like an asshole. It sounded really hot. That was before fuzz became a big deal.'

Brian decided against releasing *Little Honda* as a single (and it was left to Gary Usher and The Hondells to gain a top ten hit with the song) instead he came up with a more complex song and one of his most inventive arrangements . . . *When I Grow Up (To Be A Man)*.

With the release of their new single and riding on the success of *I Get Around* The Beach Boys made their first trip to England. Basically a promotional visit, they did, however, make an appearance on the pop-

ular TV show *Ready, Steady, Go* where they played live versions of *I Get Around* and (after a false start) *When I Grow Up*. Maybe the false start — the bum note was more a sign of stress rather than simply nerves. Whatever, things behind the scenes in The Beach Boys camp were becoming as complicated as Brian's songs. For quite a while the relationship between the group and their father-manager Murry Wilson was pretty shakey . . . For in the era of Epstein, Oldham and Grossman — Wilson senior's management approach could have been interpreted as a little quaint or even Dickensian. As Murry once told reporters, 'I have a very successful system. For acts of disobedience the boys must pay fines — ranging from 25 dollars to 200 dollars — according to the offence.'

The ties that bind finally split. Brian: 'We changed from our father to outside management basically because of the emotional strain we were under. We didn't feel that we were driving things we should have been since we are in a golden position to progress and become possibly more successful. We felt that even though my father had his heart behind it and had good intentions, because of the situation you get into between father and son, you just seem to go nowhere. It's an emotional struggle, and that's more or less a crippled situation. So we eliminated it. It was done more or less maturely. Finally, we decided he is better as a father, not a manager.'

Murry's wife Audree later remembered the incident when she told *Rolling Stone*: 'It destroyed Murry, but I understand perfectly why they did it. He was destroyed by that, and yet he wasn't really up to it. He'd already had an ulcer, and it was really too much for him, but he loved them so much. He was overly protective really, he couldn't let them go. He couldn't stand seeing anyone else handling his kids.'

Back on the US charts The Beach Boys released *Four By The Beach Boys* an extended play that featured four cuts from their *All Summer Long* album — two of the tracks *Wendy* and *Little Honda* made the top hundred in their own right. However, the group's new single *Dance, Dance, Dance*, quickly climbed into the top ten. I personally remember the disc as being something

**Below: Perched upon a UK dragster, Al looked uncomfortable and far from home on their first UK promotional visit.**



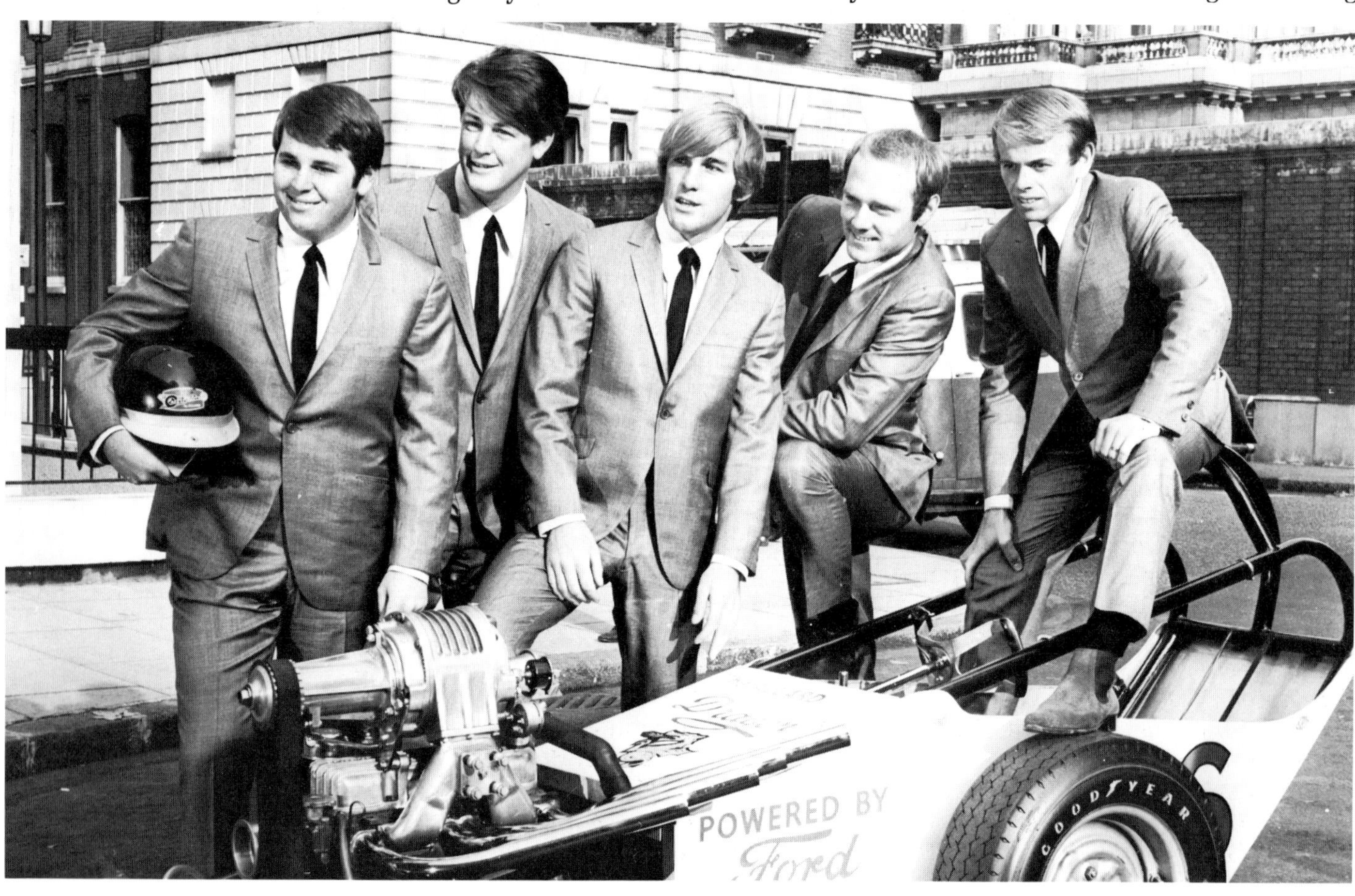

**Left: Jan Berry, 'Here they are, the one and only, the five and only, The Beach Boys.' From The Tami Show (1965).**



of a milestone. At the time I was a member of the Cardiff group The Surfbeats and seemed to be always plugging the merits of The Beach Boys to my contemporaries. Unfortunately, most of my enthusiasm fell on deaf ears. Then one evening I bumped into one such contemporary, Andy Fairweather-Low who was at the time a member of The Sect Maniacs and almost completely hooked on soul and the Stax label in particular.

He seemed quite enthused: 'You know all this Beach Boys stuff you've been on about,' he said. 'Well I was down at the Charles St Discotheque last night . . . and between the Temps' and Otis Redding they played The Beach Boys' *Dance, Dance, Dance* . . . It was great, like a breath of fresh air.' Andy later began to sound more like Carl Wilson (at times) than Carl Wilson.

Carl, by the way, co-wrote the song with Brian and his scorching twelve-string Rikenbaker contributed greatly to its solid pace. Brain: 'When I sit down at the piano and play a new song, the others can visualize the whole arrangement right away. We take the melody apart and work it out phrase by phrase. If they don't like my approach, they suggest another. If Carl doesn't dig my idea, I'll change it immediately because Carl has exquisite musical taste. I trust it completely.'

The group performed *Dance, Dance, Dance* along with *Surfin' U.S.A.* and *I Get Around* in the rock movie extravaganza *The T.A.M.I. Show* (1965) . . . Roger Christian: 'Brian was nervous but when Mike Love introduced everybody, Brian got more of an ovation than anybody, and he was just aglow . . . That was a genuine thrill at the time.'

Sadly, through contractual difficulties, The Beach Boys sequence was later dropped from the original movie.

Before the end of '64 the group released two more albums, *The Beach Boys Concert* and *The Beach Boys Christmas Album*. *The Concert* album was recorded on 1st August '64 at the Sacramento Civic Auditorium; 'before thousands of shouting, screaming

Beach Boys fans!' The album soon became a watershed in the group's career, firstly by becoming their first number one album and secondly it seemed to sum-up their recent history. With a programme that included such surf and hot rod favourites as *Hawaii*, *Little Deuce Coupe* and even Dick Dale's *Let's Go Trippin'*. They also recorded live versions of their latest hits *Fun, Fun, Fun* and *I Get Around* but, for my money I was glad to see them tipping their hats to a couple of the groups that influenced them . . . The Rivingtons, *Papa-Omm-Mow-Mow* and, of course, the great Four Freshmen classic *Graduation Day*. Unfortunately, *The Christmas Album* failed to gain anywhere near the same chart impact as *The Concert*.

Although it did herald a couple of new departures . . . For the first time on record Brian and the group teamed up with a forty-piece orchestra under the direction of Dick Reynolds, while the track *Christmas Day* marked the first recorded solo by Al Jardine.

The firing of Murry and the commercial failure of *The Christmas Album* weren't the only problems the group faced as '64 ebbed into the sunset. Brian married Marilyn Rovell on 7 December and shortly after the wedding The Beach Boys left for a short tour of the Southwest. Unhappy at the

**Rehearsing for an upcoming show 'What say we go over the ending of *Little Deuce Coupe*, one more time'. Clockwise: Big brother Brian fills in the instruments with the bass, Denny on the drums, Mike steps up to the microphone, while Al and Carl fill in on guitars.**

prospect of leaving his newly-married wife and under the constant pressure of writing, producing and performing Brian had a breakdown. Al Jardine: 'Brian decided to give up touring because he wasn't writing like he should have been.' But as Brian told Earl Leaf in '66: 'We were on tour December twenty-third. I said goodbye to Marilyn. We weren't getting along too good. The plane had been in the air only five minutes. I told Al Jardine that I was going to crack up any minute. He told me to cool it. Then I started crying. I put a pillow over my face and began screaming and yelling. Then I started telling people I'm not getting off the plane . . . started to get far out, coming undone, having a breakdown, and I just let myself go completely.'

Brian couldn't carry on with the tour, and their road manager Dick Cummings, took him back to LA. Audree Wilson: 'I met Brian at the airport, and we got in the car.' Brian requested that they should go to the house at Hawthorne, which the Wilson's still owned although they were living in Wiltshire. At the house Brian cried and poured out his problems on a sympathetic shoulder.

Marilyn: 'You know, Brian was frustrated a lot, just because of his mind. He was so sharp, and he would always get into things more . . . The music business used to get him down. You know. I used to say to him, don't worry baby.'

Brian's breakdown seemed to be a combination of things, mainly his creative abilities, how could he cope with such competitive rivals as The Beatles who saw '64 out with no less than six number one hit singles, compared to The Beach Boys one. Brian: 'We were threatened by the whole thing.' Brian also noted at the close of '64 that 'there were four Beach Boys on the road . . . they finished that tour without me. When they came back, I didn't want to talk to them or anybody. I just wanted to sit and think and rest, pull myself together, check my life out, and once again evaluate what I am, what I'm doing, and what I should be doing.'

For Brian realized that to stay in the running was not only a competition between The Beach Boys and The Beatles, but a whole new rock movement headed by Bob Dylan.

# Drag City: *Competition on the tracks*

*Well, I'm not braggin', Babe, so don't put me down*
*But I've got the fastest wheels in town*

*Little Deuce Coupe* — Wilson/Christian

**Rayner Banham summed it up best when he wrote: 'The automobile as artwork is almost specific to the Los Angeles freeways as is the surfboard to the Los Angeles beaches.'**

**Los Angeles started with surf music in 1961, but by '63, with the discovery that a teenager's first love is his car (and autos can travel longer than a wave), came hot-rod music.**

Most surf groups (and especially Brian Wilson), came under a lot of criticism for not personally participating in the sport. But, who among the bunch didn't enjoy and own a fast car. Dennis Wilson (although a real surfer), owned his fair share of fast autos in his own words: 'They say I live a fast life. Maybe I just like a fast life of driving my Stingray and X.K.E.' While Jan Berry purchased a new Stingray from 1962 to '66 and ended-up at Deadman's Curve in a shiny Corvette. If there was such a thing as a truly authentic hot-rod, drag music act, then the honour surely falls on Mr Gasser and The Weirdos. Mr Gasser and the group produced a number of albums on Capitol Records including *Surfink* and *Rods and Ratfinks.* Under the direction of Jim Economides, the line-up included Steve

Douglas, Bob and Peter Klimes, Gary Usher and ensemble and the voice of Ed 'Big Daddy' Roth.

Ed Roth was a larger than life character on the hot rod customizing scene, and he was also well into merchandizing. He not only illustrated his own album sleeve's but came up with the idea of screenprinting *Weirdo* and *Monster* T-shirts incorporating Frankenstein monsters and hot rod imagery against slogans that read *Born to Loose* or *Mother Is Wrong* etc.

Ed took mechanical drawing at East Los Angeles Junior College and UCLA, before opening his own body-shop (which he preferred to call his studio), at Maywood. Ed's motto was: 'Hell, if a guy wants to go, let him go.' Or as he told Tom Wolfe for *Esquire* magazine 'Kids love dragging a car — I mean they really love it. And what they love most is when they shift from low to second. They get to they can practically feel the rpm's. They can shift without hardly hitting the clutch at all.'

Apart from the microphone, Ed's biggest weapon was his airbrush, which he used to adorn some of his greatest creations, such as *The Rotar*, *The Beatnik Bandit* (a highly customized '32 Ford Roadster) and *The Mysterious* — a bubble top coupe powered by two 406 horsepower Thunderbird engines.

Ed, himself came on as a kinda' Ho-Dad character complete with a full beard and a tattoo on his arm, which read 'Roth'. As Ed explained to Tom: 'I had that done a couple of years ago because guys keep coming up to me saying "Are you Ed Roth?".' He went on to say: 'We are the real gangsters of the hot-rod field. They keep telling us we have a rotten attitude. We have a different attitude, but that doesn't make us rotten.'

Attitudes became indifferent to Mr Gasser's third Capitol album: *Hot Rod Hootenanny* although it included such highlights as *Eefen It Don't Chrome It*, *Termites In My Woodie* and *My Coupe Eefen Talks*.

Weirdo, Steve Douglas also recorded a host of Capitol hot rod tracks under the pseudonym Shutdown Douglas. While Capitol Records took the genre a step further by sending a recording crew under

the expertise of Jim Economides to record first-hand the burnin' rubber of *The Big Sounds of The Drags Vols I* and *II* . . . from the strip itself.

The two discs that, however, injected fresh fuel into the auto-crowd and record buyers alike were The Rip Chords with *Hey Little Cobra* and Ronny and The Daytonas' *G.T.O.*

The Rip Chords were the brainchild of Californian duo Bruce Johnston and Terry Melcher. Bruce was a neighbour of Jan Berry and often played piano for Jan's group The Barons.

It was at one of The Barons practice sessions that Dean Torrence introduced Bruce to drummer Sandy Nelson and they soon began working together in various groups and recording sessions.

The first disc they cut was as members of Skip Tyler and The Flips; released on the Ebb label — *She's My Witch* coupled with *Rumble Rock* failed to make an impression on the charts.

A short time later, they formed The Sleepwalkers with Phil Spector and Richie Podolor but again failed to get anything off the ground. Johnston: 'I even used to be in a band with Phil Spector. We played high school dances together, though not for long. But I knew he had it together, 'cause he was playing on demos.

He asked the drummer on the band if I would come and play on a demo and I didn't 'cause I was busy that night — had a date or something, and I wasn't old enough to drive, so I had to be driven wherever I had to go. So I didn't make the session, and it turned out to be his first hit with the Teddy Bears, *To Know Him, Is to Love Him*. I'm not that old, but I've been doing it for so long. I used to back Richie Valens up when he was very big in the States, and that drummer Sandy Nelson. He asked me to go on the road with the Big Bopper, Buddy Holly and Richie Valens, you know when they had the fatal plane crash?

My Ma wouldn't let me go on tours. I was too young . . . Of course, nothing would have happened to me, 'cause I wouldn't have been on that plane. So that night after they died, Bobby Valino (Vee) stood in for Holly and that's when he got his start. A year later I played his show."

Bruce and Sandy also found plenty of work as Hollywood session musicians. While on a session with Original Sound, Sandy asked if he could record a little drum number called *Teen Beat*. He made the disc and it soared into the top ten. Bruce played on *Big Jump* the discs flip-side but after the records huge success their partnership ceased. On the strength of *Teen Beat*, Nelson was invited in '59 to appear on Dick Clark's *American Bandstand* before touring America and Europe. He later went over to Imperial and recorded more hits including *Let There Be Drums, Drums Are My Beat* and *Drummin' Up A Storm*. Just before Sandy Nelson split for the big time, he recorded a couple of instrumentals *Charge* and *Geronimo* as The Renegades with Bruce. Interesting, the songwriting credits went to one Nik Venet and they along with *Because of You*, written by Bruce were included on the soundtrack of the movie *The Ghost of Dragstrip Hollow* (1959).

Bruce carried on writing songs while also forming Bruce and Jerry (the Jerry being one Jerry Cooper). They had a number of unsuccessful singles released on the Arwin Label — where probably Bruce first met Terry, as Terry's mum and dad owned the label. Terry Melcher had the ultimate

Southern Californian childhood, the only son of Doris Day he grew-up in Beverly Hills romping under the watchful eyes of neighbours like Patte Page.

While at High School, he took a summer job at Pacific Ocean Park, an amusement arcade where his speciality was scaring patrons of the Sky Bubble by convincingly feigning distress. After attending college at Principia (a Christian Science establishment) he made his first disc in 1961 under the name Terry Day — 'Carrying on in a great tradition' — cried the music trade publications. But, the music was rock 'n' roll produced by Phil Spector. Melcher: 'Columbia hadn't heard of Spector. Somehow I convinced them he was all the rage. He spent fifteen thousand on the first song, plus his airfare and hotel. I made that last for three months. I was terrible, actually. Then I left Columbia for a year and a half, until I came back as an office boy.' Terry joined Columbia's New York office under his step-father's name and has continued to use it ever since.

Bruce at this time, was working as a producer at Bob Keene's Del-Fi Records, and the first act Keene entrusted to young Bruce was singer Ron Holden.

Keene was on a promotional visit at Washington State in 1960 when he heard Holden's *Love You So*, a local-radio hit. He immediately bought the rights from the local Night Owl label and distributed the disc nationwide on his newly-formed Donna Label (named after the Ritchie Valens hit). *Love You So*, became number seven in the nation. Bruce co-wrote and produced Holden's next four singles, plus an album. However, they never managed to repeat the success of *Love You So*.

Then in February '62, Johnston discovered on his very own beach front . . . surfing music . . . released on Donna under his own name came *Do The Surfer Stomp Parts I* and *II* soon to be followed by *The Original Surfer Stomp* on Del-Fi. Johnston's first album was released by Del-Fi in June '63, titled *The Bruce Johnston Surfing Band: Surfers Pyjama Party* it included such rock standards as Wilbert Harrison's *Kansas City*, Booker T & The MG's *Green Onions* and Ray Charles' *What'd I Say* — a not very inspiring first effort, apart from (perhaps)

**Left: A scene from *The Ghost of Dragstrip Hollow* (1959).**

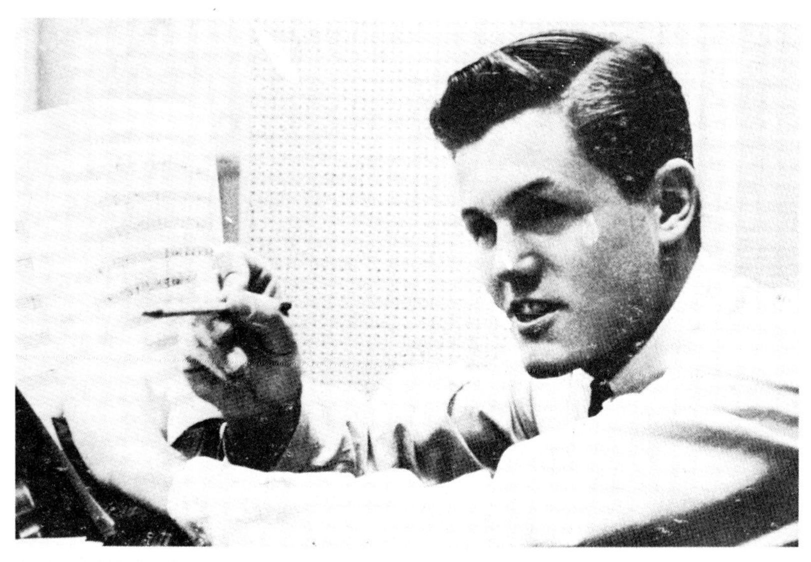

**Above: Top, Bruce during the *Surfin' Round The World* session. Below: Bruce aboard probably the world's largest woodie.**

*Something On Your Mind* which was recorded live at the Sigma P: Fraternity House UCLA. Although it quickly led-on to better things. Terry Melcher returned to the coast after serving his apprenticeship in New York. While at Fun City he spent much time at the offices of music publisher Don Kirshner, famous for its stable of young hit-makers including Neil Sedaka, Carole King and Gerry Goffin.

Melcher: 'The greatest moment of my life was loaning my sports coat to Gerry Goffin.' Being around such songwriters made a great impression on the young Terry.

Back in LA, he was soon hired by David Kapralik, head of A&R at Columbia Records, as one of a group of ambitious producers whom the company hoped would improve its position in the singles charts.

One of the first artists he worked with was Frankie Laine, who hadn't had a hit since '57, by the time his *Don't Make My Baby Blue* rose into the top fifty, Terry had renewed his acquaintance with Bruce Johnston and had also realized the potential in the surfing craze.

Bruce was billed as 'A New Star on Columbia Records'; and Terry produced his first album for the label . . . *Surfin' Round The World* . . . although the album never became a smash hit, it did include a couple of surf classics (including Bruce's own *Jersey Channel Islands Part I*).

For their second surfin' outing, they became The Hot Doggers on the summer of '63 *Surfin' U.S.A.* album.

Apart from their covers of The Beach Boys' title song *Surfin'* and *Surfin' Safari*, the duo produced adequate versions of such surf instrumentals as *Miserlou*, *Pipeline*, *Surfer's Stomp* and *Let's Go Trippin'*.

At this time, Terry was also busy with another studio creation, The Rip Chords. Basically a bunch of session musicians, the group consisted of Ernie Bringas, Phil Stewart, Glen Campbell and Hal Blaine.

Bringas grew up in the LA suburb of Inglewood and attended school with his friend Phil Stewart. While at school the duo became determined to break into the record business. After a few years without any luck, they were both beginning to give up on their dream when . . . Bringas: 'Then I was going through some of my old records and noticed a couple by Jan and Arnie on the Arwin label (published by Daywin Music Inc.) and since they had left the label (and publishing company), I thought that maybe Daywin might need someone to replace them. I took in a dub to Bob Crystal who was Vice President of the company — who later was to become our manager and he liked it.

He called me a couple of days later and said they wanted the song, which was called *Raindrops*, for Doris Day to record — we were pleased that they liked the song, but disappointed that they didn't want us to sing it.'

Although Doris Day never recorded the song, she played the demo to her son Terry and he asked the duo to come down to Columbia and audition for him. Ernie: 'We went in an auditioned for Terry Melcher and a couple of days later we got a phone call saying "Welcome to Columbia Records".

Their first disc *Here I Stand* was produced by Melcher with a Jack Nitzsche arrangement and featured Glen Campbell on guitar and Hal Blaine on drums, the latter session crew would feature on all The Rip Chords product.

Terry: 'It's a jive job being a record producer. You really have to presume a lot. You take it upon yourself to decide, is this a good guitar break? Should it be done again? Is that bass part strong enough? Because the people who are playing don't ever want to say, "That's the best I can do." Never in your life will you hear that. All you'll ever hear is, "I can do it better."'

For their second single *Gone* (co-written by Johnston and Melcher), both Terry and Bruce helped out on the background singing parts. Bringas: 'Terry never thought he could sing, but we were messing around in the studio one day and discovered he had a really good sound.

So we got him and Bruce to sing on the record, but since they were too busy with their production duties to tour as The Rip Chords and I couldn't tour because I was in school, Phil hired two musicians — Arnie Marcus and Rich Rotkin — to tour with him and The Rip Chords for personal appearances.'

From this disc on Bruce and Terry both played a bigger part in the group's recorded sound and chose for their third single *Hey Little Cobra*. Released in November '64 the disc with its flip-side, Melcher and Johnston's *The Queen* rose straight into the national top five.

*Cobra* was written by Carol Conners (originally known as Annette Kleinbard of The Teddy Bears fame). She also contributed to many other hot rod tunes, including Dick Dale's *Blond In The 406* and *My X-K-E* (co-written with Steve Barri), The Zipcodes, *Run Little Mustang* and, again, The Rip Chord's *Red Hot Roadster*. *Roadster* performed by The Rip Chords was featured in the movie *A Swingin' Summer* ('65) a strip of celluloid, more famous for introducing TV's *Hollywood Palace* billboard girl, Raquel Welch to the big screen.

As one half of Carol and Cheryl (the Cheryl being her sister), she had an unsuccessful run at the charts with *Go, Go, GTO* coupled with *Sunny Weather* on Colpix in February '65.

Carol also teamed with Roger Christian on a number of songs, again without the same impact as *Hey Little Cobra* had on the record buying public. For their first outing in '64, The Rip Chords released Jan Berry and Roger Christian's *Three Window Coupe* and it finally peaked at the number twenty eight position. Perhaps more interesting was its flip side *Hot Rod USA* written by Melcher and the multi-talented Bobby Darin. Darin, real name Walden Robert Cassotto, first broke into the charts in '58 with *Splish Splash* quickly followed by *Queen of The Hop*, *Plain Jane* and *Dream Lover*. He carried on his hit-making run throughout the next decade while also becoming a highly rated screen actor.

**Below: Bobby Darin, hot-rod enthusiast and co-writer of *Hot Rod USA* and *Boss Barracuda*.**

Official Souvenir Program 50¢

presents

# A MILLION DOLLAR PARTY

... IN PERSON:

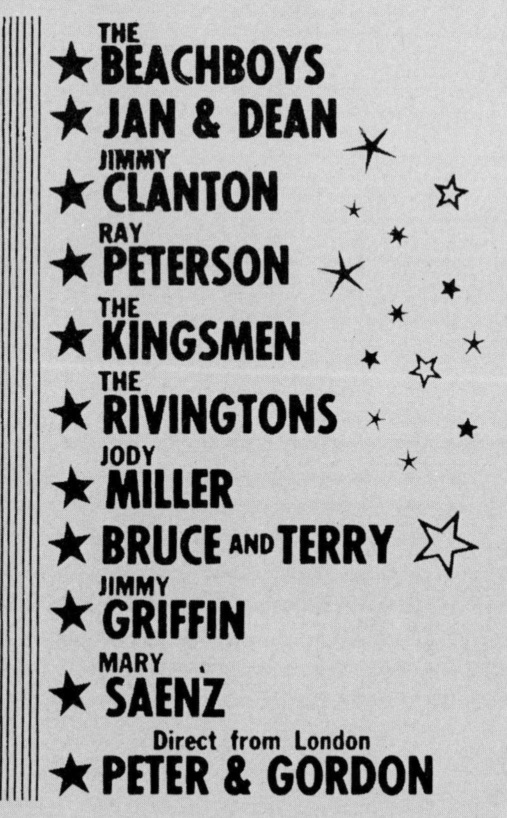


WITH THE K-poi ALL STARS
featuring
PHIL SLOAN • GLENN CAMPBELL
and
HAL "Drummer Man" BLAINE

TOM MOFFATT, M.C.

JULY 3 & 4, 1964
HONOLULU
INTERNATIONAL CENTER ARENA

Bobby also had a real passion for exotic autos and even commissioned Kustom King, George Barris to apply his famous 'diamond-rust' paint job to his Andy DiDia specially designed streamlined *Dream Car*.

Terry and Bobby also collaborated on *Boss Barracuda* a song that's lyrics seemed to say it all:

*Buddy you can brag about your Thunderbird,*
*And your Three Window Coupe around Dead Man's Curve*
*But, you can't boss my Boss Barracuda around.*

Both tunes contained the necessary melody, drive and sunny harmonies that soon enticed other acts (including The Knights and The Surfaris) to cover them. Two months prior to The Rip Chord's *Three Window Coupe* release, Bruce and Terry for the first time as a team took the spotlight (as Bruce and Terry) and put-out a cover of The Beach Boy's *Custom Machine* it crept into the hot hundred. They followed up their mini success with *Summer Means Fun* in July '64 and in the same month appeared on stage together for a two day set of concerts at the Honolulu International Center Arena along with The Beach Boys, Jan and Dean and others. This live-Honolulu soíree caused stage-shy Melcher's early retirement from public performance. Back at the mixing desk, Terry became even more ambitious and looked for a more established artiste to produce, he found one, in

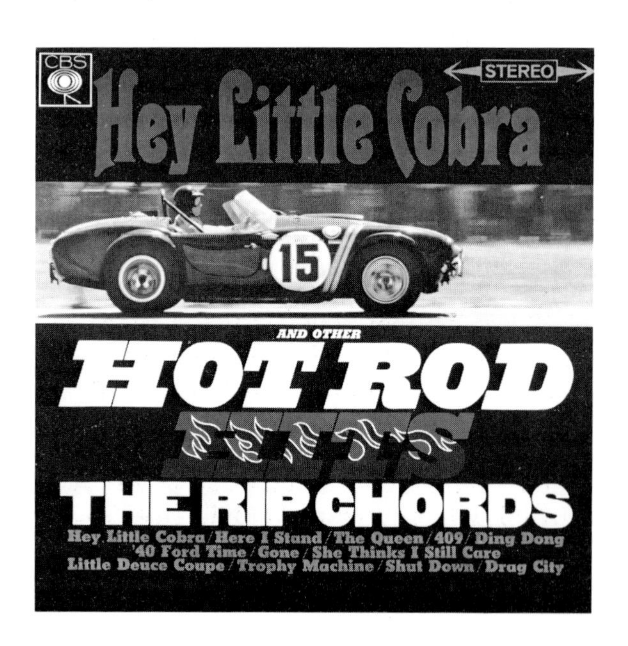

the form of 50's hearthrob Pat Boone. Melcher: 'I cut Pat Boone for Dot. A song called *Little Honda* that Brian wrote. I cut the track when Pat Boone was in Las Vegas and I took the track there to add his voice to it. Meanwhile, I'd made a demo for him so he could learn the tune. Bruce and I had put all The Beach Boy's parts on it already and all Pat had to do was a few "I'm gonna wake you up earlys" and it was covered. If he got through about fifteen words and sounded like Mike Love, I figured it was top ten.

'I got to Pat's hotel in Vegas. We were gonna do it between shows; there's a United Recorders about a mile from the Strip. I knew Usher had been cutting the same tune; I knew it would be close. Pat came up to his room to change. They had piped-in radio in the suite. I'm waiting while he puts on his shirt. I've got the lead sheets, I've got my eight track tape, he's buttoning his shirt and the record comes on the radio, Usher's record! I didn't know what to do; just didn't know what to do. And he was kinda . . . singing along with it for a couple of minutes! Then he said, "Hey! wait a minute! what's that?" I did some incredible double talk.

I said "It's an unknown group Pat, we'll have no trouble getting the airplay, your momentum will carry us" (he hadn't had a hit in like seven years). Anyway, the back side of the record was a version of *Beach Girl* which we also did with/as The Rip Chords. And Dot sold a hundred thousand copies of the single.' After the running success of The Hondell's version, most jocks flipped the disc and *Beach Girl* landed at number seventy two — nineteen places higher than Pat's previous single. Both sides of the single were produced by Melcher and Johnston. While *Beach Girl* was also written by the duo and appeared on The Rip Chord's second album . . . *Three Window Coupe.*

Staying with the four-wheel genre, Ronny and The Daytonas, although based in Nashville, Tennessee; out of all the non-Californian surf and hot rod groups they became the most consistent hit makers in the field.

The group was the brainchild of Ronny Daytona (real name John Bucky Wilkin) the son of singer-songwriter Marijohn Wilkin whose song *Long Black Veil* appeared on The Band's debut album, *Music From The Big Pink.*

Ronny & The Daytonas themselves were a very loose outfit. Wilkin: 'They were just friends of mine who were also in the record business. There was Bobby Russell who was a songwriter, Buzz Cason who was a producer and writer, and Bergen White who was an arranger and say maybe half a dozen others, who were say exchangeable. I'd play on their records and they'd play on mine and so we never did have a set group of relatives like The Beach Boys. We just had a few friends who worked on each other's things.'

Other featured players included Johnny Johnson; lead guitar and vocals, Van Evans; bass and vocals and Lynn Williams on drums. The group signed to the local Amy/Mala label early in '64 and put under the production direction of veteran Bill Justis of *Raunchy* fame.

Their first release, the John Wilkin penned *G.T.O.* raced up the charts to finally take the flag at the number four position in

**Far left: The programme from Bruce and Terry's only live performance.**

**Right: The promising producer Terry Melcher.**

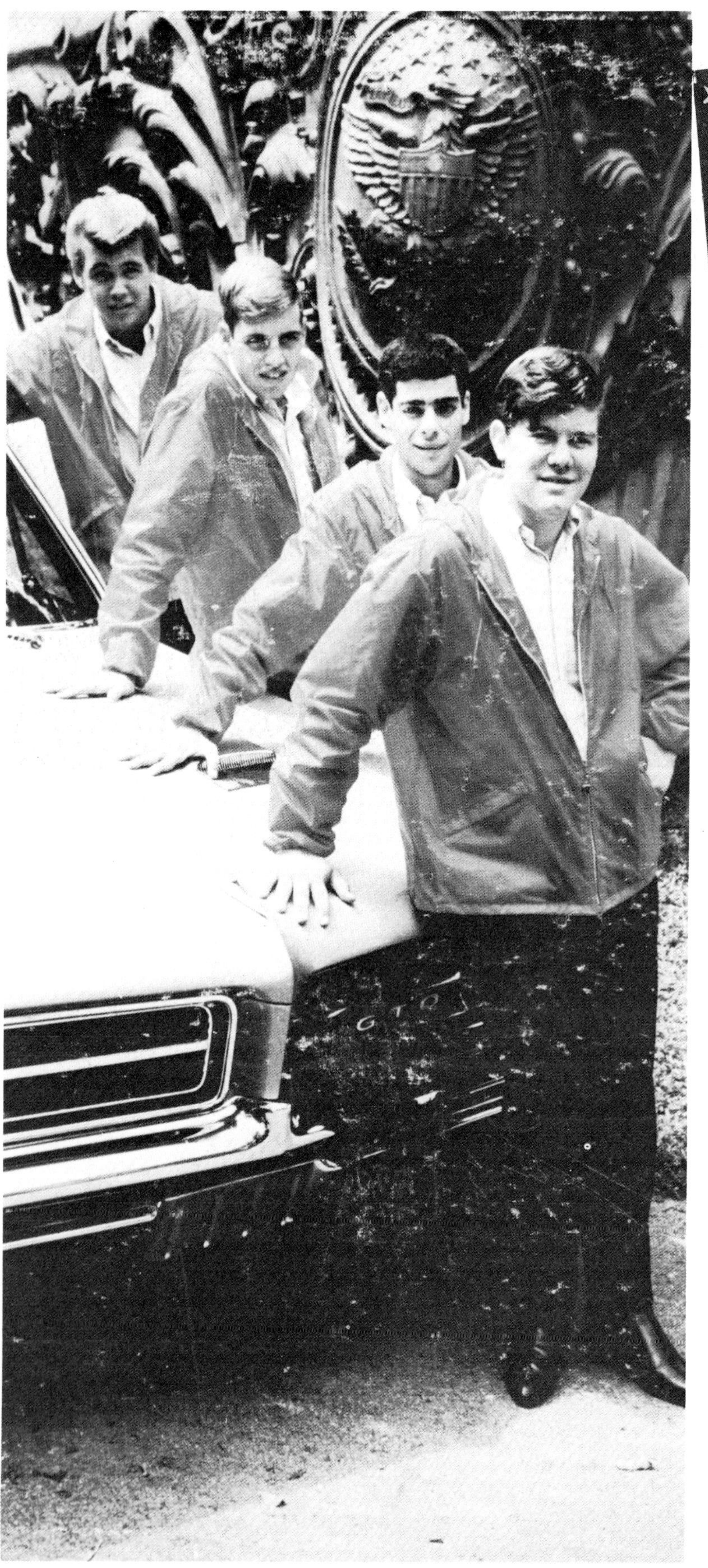

August '64. The disc had a full and solid sound, the perfect combination of Chuck Berry and The Beach Boys.

By their sound, most punters believed the Southern boys were pure West Coast. Wilkin: 'I didn't really try to get anything across. It sort of just fell together. But there's a lot of people go down to Florida — Daytona in Florida (hence the name) and there's like a lot of surfing and hot rods down there (Daytona Beach and Daytona Speedway), which as you know is pretty close to Tennessee.'

Their next single *California Bound* seemed to sum-up their predicament . . . another Wilkin original, unfortunately it lost power at number seventy two in the charts. Although they did use the track to open their debut album, *G.T.O.* The album was packed with goodies including *Hot Rod Baby, Little Rail Job, Surfin' In The Summertime, Hot Rod City, Antique '32 Studebaker Dictator Coupe* (a difficult one to say, let alone sing), plus their next single *Bucket "T"*.

Roger Christian, who co-wrote the song with Jan Berry, Dean Torrence and Don Altfeld offered them the song. Wilkin: 'It was an album cut and we were the first to put it out as a single I believe.' It quickly rose into the National top fifty firmly establishing them as one of the leading exponents of hot rod music.

Their next couple of singles failed to gain any major chart placings, although, *Beach Boy* coupled with *No Wheels* gained a lot of airplay. Both sides, were co-written by Buzz Cason who not only supplied Jan and Dean with their *Tennessee* and *Popsicle* hits but was also responsible for The Eliminators; *Liverpool, Dragsters, Cycles & Surfing* album and The Zip-Code's *Mustang* album . . . both albums were released on Liberty Records. Liberty Records became one of the major outlets for hot rod music, apart from the above mentioned and the Jan and Dean product they also released a string of albums by The T. Bones. Produced by Dave Pell and arranged by Perry 'Bunny' Botkin (who later produced Harry Nilsson's *Pandemonium Shadow Show* album), The T. Bones were basically a (sax orientated) set of studio musicians who covered hot rod hits such as *Little Deuce Coupe, Drag City* and *Hey Little Cobra* in an instrumental style.

The above titles featured on their *Boss Drag* album. Although the album failed to set the charts ablaze it did, however, become a steady seller and The T. Bones were soon back in the studio putting together a more original set. Released as *Boss Drag At The Beach*, apart from the host of new tunes it also featured The Rip Chords, *Hot Rod U.S.A.* and Usher and Christian's *Competition Coupe*.

*Competition Coupe* also became the title of The Astronauts hot rod album. Released on RCA, it included seven cover versions from The Vettes *Rev-Up* album. The Vettes were a studio creation put together by ex-Beach Boys' producer Nick Venet and included Steve Douglas on sax and Bruce Johnston on organ and lead vocals.

Steve Douglas, under the alias Shutdown Douglas, also helped to fill out a number of Capitol Hot Rod albums and never sounded better than on his *Wipe Outish, Twin Cut-Outs*. Capitol Records took more than their fair share of the hot rod album chart honours, The Beach Boys' *Little Deuce Coupe* and *Shut Down Vol. II*; Dick Dale's *Checkered Flag* and *Mr. Eliminator* and The Knight's *Hot Rod High*, just to name a few. While producer Jim Econimedes (who was responsible for the last three albums), carried on his pit stop sessions with *The History of Drag Racing* and *Breedlove — 500*.

Back on the musical front, Jerry Cole who recorded a number of surf instrumental albums (with his group The Spacemen) under Economedes production for Capitol, changed his surname initial, his group name and label and released Jerry Kole and the Strokers *Hot Rod Alley* album on Crown.

But out of all the hot rod instrumentalists, one of the most popular in and around the LA area was Jim Messina and The Jesters. Although, their debut single — the Latin influenced *The Breeze and I* had little or nothing to do with the scorching sounds usually associated with the genre . . . their album *The Dragsters* was packed with high powered energy and included eight original tracks co-written by Messina and Glenn Frey. Unfortunately, the album like so many of their contemporaries, did little outside of the Southern California area. Lillian Roxan in her Encyclopedia of Rock really put the record straight when she wrote 'The hot-rod sound was quite similar to the surf sound, very California and summery, and naturally easy to drive to.'

**Far left: Ronny (John Bucky Wilkin) leading The Daytonas.**

# Celluloid Surf: *Cinema City on the crest of the wave*

*Come on everybody grab your baggies and bikinis*
*Cause' the party has just begun.*

*Summer Means Fun* — Phil Sloan/Steve Barri

**Annette Funicello shook off her Mickey Mouse ears, squeezed into a one-piece bathing costume and with her burgeoning voluptuousness graced the set for the start of a series of sunny, sandy and soppy shindings . . . The beach movie had truly arrived.**

Shortly after *Gidget* left the shore, packed her bags and headed for Italy. American International Pictures hired director William Asher, a film crew, Annette, Philly popster Frankie Avalon, a group of surfers, a supporting cast of beefies in bathers and bikinis plus a number of local surf acts and banished them to a Hollywood backlot — and on occasion Malibu Beach to film *Beach Party* (1963).

Written and produced by Lou Rusoff and James H. Nicholson, the movie became a great success and created a formula that would be followed and copied for the next three years.

Annette: 'It was like being on summer vacation everyday of the year. It was some of the most fun I've ever had. Working with good buddy Frankie Avalon made it extra nice, and the surfers were fun too.'

Annette had been chief Mousketeer in the long-running TV series *The Mickey Mouse Show* (1955/59), and soon progressed into full feature films including *The Shaggy Dog* (1961) and *Babes In Toyland* (1961). While also notching up a number of hit singles her biggest being *Tall Paul* which made number seven in January '59.

So, at the age of twenty, she was a natural to play the role of Dee Dee the long suffering girlfriend of Frankie (Frankie Avalon).

By the time Avalon arrived on the Beach Party Set, clad in baggies, he'd already had a long and distinguished record and movie career.

Starting with his first hit single *De De Dinah* in '58, he soon gained his first number one hit *Venus* in February '59.

The following year he made his screen debut opposite Alan Ladd in *The Guns of*

*Timberland* (1960), quickly followed by *The Alamo* (1960), starring and directed by John Wayne. Forgetting the lack of bleached blonde hair, Avalon seemed the perfect choice to play the softhearted romantic lead.

Between their romantic escapades, Frankie, Dee Dee and their surfing buddies always found plenty of antagonism from pint-sized beach bully Eric Von Zipper (Sgt Bilko's Harvey Lembeck) and his black denim ho-dad crew.

Although Frankie seemed to find more action with the stream of young nubiles who would frequent their beach including, Linda Evans, Eva Six and Luciana Paluzzi (to the dismay of Dee Dee) than with Von Zipper's greasers.

For there always seemed to be a beachload of scantily clad young ladies around even if they were only extras. Annette: 'I was still under contract to Walt Disney, and he had full script approval. He said, "I don't mind you wearing a two-piece, but I would prefer you not showing the navel!" So respecting him as I did, that was fine with me. It didn't matter.'

Another young startlet of the series, Donna Loren, who was also an ex-Mousketeer shared Mr Disney's moralistic views completely and was even labelled by *Saturday Evening Post* as "The Nellie Melba of the beach movies." (Miss Melba was the prima donna of Australian opera at the turn of the century and was famous for being prim, proper, talented and adored by her fans.)

Donna of the beach bunny lib once stated: 'The other people are screamed at and scratched apart; but me, nobody grabs me. They just stand and wait with all the respect in the world. I'm on a pedestal — I don't believe in going up there and sticking a bikini on and shaking around.'

Loren (or Donna Zukor) had made several discs and TV appearances before she was chosen by John Simmons an advertising vice president as the *Dr. Pepper*'s girl.

She appeared regularly on Dick Clark's *Bandstand*, sponsoring the soft drink that in turn led to a contract with AIP.

Capitol Records Voyle Gilmore spotted her in '64 while she was opening a Dick Dale concert at the Aragon Ballroom, Los

**AIP's beach party line-up. Front row, Candy Johnson, John Ashley, Frankie Avalon and Annette Funicello.**

Angeles. Gilmore: 'I was sitting in the audience when Donna came on to sing. In thirty years of watching performers I have never seen one to match her stage presence and ability to capture attention. The amazing thing is that this same rapport is evident on her records.'

Back on the beach . . . If Annette couldn't and Donna wouldn't who were they talking about in the publicity handout for AIP's second seaside outing . . . 'When 10,000 biceps go round 5,000 bikinis . . . you know what's gonna happen at . . . Muscle Beach Party.'

One thing is for sure, dancer Candy Johnson wasn't perturbed about wobbling her tanned tummy to a dance step she dubbed the *Ebb 'n' Flow*. A regular player in the AIP beach series Candy also released an album with The Exciters, *The Candy Johnson Show at Bikini Beach* on the local Canjo label.

*Muscle Beach Party* (1964) also introduced Little Stevie Wonder to the big screen, as Scott St James noted: 'He appears in *Muscle Beach Party*, that was released by American International Pictures, and his immediate successes in this media have led to further offers from movieland. But the final Wonder of it all — his single release on the Tamla label, *Castles In The Sand*, received widespread acclaim and acceptance from the legions of fans for a performance in a field partially new to him, the surfing sound, done in his own ballad style' . . . Stevie Wonder was into surf music? Co-

**Above: Little Stevie Wonder. Below: Burnin' rubber . . . Annette. Opposite top: A well padded Frankie in search of a Ski Party.**

star Jody McCrea (son of Western star Joel) who played the character Deadhead also released a surf single *Chicken Surfer* on the Canjo label in '64. While Stevie turned up again in *Bikini Beach* ('64) performing *Fingertips*. However, the bona fide surf stars were in abundance throughout the AIP beach series. *Beach Party* found Dick Dale and The Deltones performing Usher and Christian's *Secret Surfin'* spot that was finally released on Capitol Records, and both Annette and Frankie Avalon had chart attempts with Usher and Christian's title song. Although there wasn't a true soundtrack album released, Funicello also released a *Beach Party* album featuring the title song, *Secret Surfin' Spot, Swingin' and Surfin'* (also an Usher and Christian song from the film) plus her great cover version of The Rivieras *California Sun*.

For *Muscle Beach Party*, Usher and Christian called in their buddy Brian Wilson to help out on the title song plus *Muscle Bustle. Muscle Bustle* was released as a single by Donna Loren, while Annette and Avalon both released *Muscle Beach Party* albums. Annette came off marginally better, for Usher and Christian supplied four new titles, *Draggin' U.S.A., Shutdown Again, Custom City* and *Rebel Rider* to help fill out the sides with authentic surf songs. Poor Ole' Frankie had to settle for minor cover versions of Henry Mancini's *Moon River* and *The Days of Wine and Roses*.

Wilson and Christian along with Jan Berry came up with their biggest surf movie song *Ride The Wild Surf* (1964) for Jan and Dean. Released by Columbia Pictures and directed by Don Taylor the movie starred Fabian, Tab Hunter and Shelly Fabares (who wasn't afraid to go two-piece). Jan and Dean were also to appear. Dean Torrance: 'Jan and I were supposed to be in this epic — our film debut co-starring with Fabian. But right about the same time a close friend of mine kidnapped Frank Sinatra Jr, so, the movie people kicked me out of the film. I think they thought that another one of my friends might try to kidnap Fabian.'

Trailing behind the golden Coppertone of the *Beach Party* series and *Ride The Wild Surf* came Maury Dexter's monotone *Surf Party* (1964). A very low-budget production its star Bobby Vinton once claimed that he was only paid $750 for his appearance.

Over at AIP they were as busy as ever. Avalon: 'I've made *Beach Party* and *Muscle Beach Party*, and the next one is *Bikini Beach Party*. After that I guess it'll be *Son of Beach Party*.' In fact it became *Beach Blanket Bingo* (1965) followed by *How to Stuff A Wild Bikini* (1965). But the strain of it all was beginning to tell. Annette: 'I was tired of wearing the heavy pancake make-up, so I decided to buy a sunlamp to get a face tan. Well, I fell asleep underneath it. The next day my eyes were glued shut, and I had these horrible blisters all over my face, but I still went to work. Because of my blisters, they still had to put on the heavy make-up. In the scene Frankie and I were driving down the highway. The wind was blowing, and my blisters started popping. Frankie didn't know about the blisters, and he started freaking out. He thought he was in a horror movie. All the beach party movies were shot in November for summer release, so it was always freezing.'

Frankie finally quit the beach and headed for the mountains for *Ski Party* (1965). Directed by Alan Rafkin and co-starring Dwayne Hickman, Deborah Walley and Yvonne Craig, the plot incorporated *Some Like It Hot* overtones with Frankie and Dwayne dressing in girls clothes in their attempt to join a womens ski-ing class and dormitory.

The Hondells performed Usher's *Ski Party* and *The Gasser*, while Annette and Gary Usher appeared in cameo roles. Usher: 'I appeared in the background in this one but I didn't receive any credit. I was over the thrill of it all by this stage and rather than freeze to death out in the snow, I was by the fire drinking hot-buttered rums and having a good time.'

Director Lennie Weinrib moved into the same area for his *Wild, Wild Winter* (1965). Starring Gary Clarke and Chris Noel the movie also featured a song from The Astronauts. Chris Noel also appeared in Weinrib's *Beach Ball* (1965), playing opposite Ed Kookie Byrnes. The movie also featured The Supremes singing the title song plus *Surfer Boy* while The Hondells performed *My Buddy Seat* and ex-Moongooners — The Walker Brothers appeared in cameo.

However, out of all the also run beach epics, *For Those Who Think Young* (1964)

probably came closest to the *Beach Party* formula. Directed by Leslie Martinson, the movie starred James Darren — returning to the beach for the first time since *Gidget Goes Hawaiian* (1961), Pamela Tiffin, Nancy Sinatra and the dependable Paul Lynde (who also portrayed Bullets throughout the *Beach Party* series).

Annette once summed up the beach party philosophy best when she told Rodney Bingenheimer; 'I think they portrayed everybody's dream of what they would like their summer vacation to be, especially those kids who didn't live near water. Their big dream was to come out to Malibu Beach and to surf and dance on the sand, and to have weenie roasts every night. It also showed you that you could have fun without using vulgar language and without explicit sex scenes.'

**Below: Surf's up in the Hollywood tank for James Darren and Pamela Tiffen.**

# *Hangin' Ten . . .*

**1. Gidget** (1959)
**Directed by:** Paul Wendkos
**Cast:** Sandra Dee, Cliff Robertson, James Darren and Doug McClure
**Featuring:** The Four Preps
**Songs include:** *Gidget, The Next Best Thing To Love* and *Cinderella.*
*Gidget* was the forerunner of a mini series *Gidget Goes Hawaiian* (1961) and *Gidget Goes To Rome* (1963) and was also the original scene setter for the beach movie genre. The movie starred Sandra Dee (in the title role) as an inexperienced surfer, who is saved from drowning by Moondoggie (Darren), thus starting a teen romance. However, complications arise in the form of beachnik Robertson who muscles in and almost steals her away.

**2. Beach Party** (1963)
**Directed by:** William Asher
**Cast:** Annette Funicello, Frankie Avalon, Harvey Lembeck, Eva Six, Jody McCrae, John Ashley and Dorothy Malone
**Featuring:** Dick Dale and The Deltones
**Songs include:** *Beach Party, Treat Him Nicely, Promise Me Anything, Don't Stop Now, Surfin' and A Swingin'* and *Secret Surfin' Spot.*
First in the long running AIP beach movies series, Beach Party added sixties gloss to the formula created by Gidget. Frankie (Avalon) plans a moonlight beach blanket session with Dee Dee (Funicello), only to find that she turns up with the rest of the gang including Deadhead (McCrae) and Johnny (Ashley) . . . and to add insult to injury wearing a one-piece.

Sharing the beach front with them, the plot includes a sympathetic anthropologist (Cummings) nicknamed Pigbristle's who spies on the young couple in order to write a book about the mating habits and teen tribalism of the Californian beach set. Eva Six adds sex appeal while ho-dad Eric Von Zipper (Lembeck) does his best to wreek havoc throughout the movie.

**3. Muscle Beach Party** (1964)
**Directed by:** William Asher
**Cast:** Annette Funicello, Frankie Avalon, Luciana Paluzzi, John Ashley, Jody McCrea, Candy Johnson, Don Rickles, Morey Amsterdam and Buddy Hackett.
**Featuring:** Little Stevie Wonder and Dick Dale and The Deltones and somewhere on the beach Brian Wilson, Gary Usher and Roger Christian (who also supplied most of the songs).
**Songs include:** *Muscle Beach Party, Happy Street, Surfers Holiday, Runnin' Wild, A Boy Needs A Girl, A Girl Needs a Boy, Muscle Bustle* and *My First Love.*
In the second AIP outing visiting Italian Countess (Paluzzi) falls for the charms of Frankie . . . then things really hot up when her former boyfriend — the muscle bound Mr Galaxy arrives on the scene. Not that there's a lot to worry about, by the final scene Frankie's back in the long suffering arms of Dee Dee. Other features include Buddy Hackett as a rich business manager, dancer Candy Johnson demonstrating a new dance step; *The Ebb 'n' Flow* and Stevie Wonder putting in a performance down at Cappy's Surf Club.

**4. Bikini Beach** (1964)
**Directed by:** William Usher.
**Cast:** Annette Funicello, Frankie Avalon, Harvey Lembeck, Keenan Wynn, John Ashley, Jody McCrea, Candy Johnson, Don Rickles, Martha Hyer and Donna Loren.
**Featuring:** Little Stevie Wonder, The Excitors and The Pyramids.
**Songs include:** *Fingertips, Bikini Beach, Midnight Run, Because You're You, This Times Its Love, How About That, Secret Weapon* and *Gimme Your Love.*
The posters screamed 'The girls are Bare-ing . . . The guys are Dar-ing and surfs Rare-ing to Go, Go, Go' . . . All this plus two Frankies for the price of one. For apart from playing his usual role, Avalon portrays Potato Bug an English rock singing-drag racer.

Bug and the usual crew help overcome the disastrous plans of property speculator Huntington Honeywagon (Wynn) who wants to take over their happy hunting ground.

**5. How To Stuff A Wild Bikini** (1965)
**Directed by:** William Asher
**Cast:** Annette Funicello, Dwayne Hickman, Buster Keaton, Mickey Rooney, Jody McCrea; Beverly Adams, John Ashley, Harvey Lombeck and Brian Donlevy.
**Featuring:** The Kingsmen, Brian Wilson and Frankie Avalon.
**Songs include:** *How To Stuff A Wild Bikini, Better Be Ready, Give Her Lovin', The Perfect Boy* and *After The Party.*
Frankie (Avalon) is called away on naval reserve duty (when infact he was on the ski-slopes filming Ski Party '65). While he's away he calls upon the services of a witch doctor (Keaton) to keep a watchful eye over Dee Dee (Annette) to make sure she remains true.

Apart from the absence of Avalon things remain the same.

**6. Beach Blanket Bingo** (1965)
**Directed by:** William Asher
**Cast:** Annette Funicello, Frankie Avalon, Buster Keaton, Donna Loren, Paul Lynde, Harvey Lembeck, John Ashley, Linda Evans, Jody McCrea and Deborah Walley.
**Featuring:** The Hondells
**Songs include:** *Beach Blanket Bingo, The Cycle Set, You'll Never Change Him, I Think, You Think, These Are The Good Times, Fly Boy, New Love, It Only Hurts When I Cry* and *I Am My Ideal.*
The gang's at it again, this time sky-diving into the waves . . . Deadhead (McCrea) is smittened by a life-saving mermaid, while Dee Dee (Annette) is completely distraught when Frankie (Avalon) falls for Sugar Kane portrayed by pre-Dynasty's Linda Evans.

As usual, by the final reel their frolics end on a happy note.

**7. Surf Party** (1964)
**Directed by:** Maury Dexter
**Cast:** Bobby Vinton, Patricia Morrow, Kenny Miller, Jackie De Shannon, Richard Crane and Lory Patrick.
**Featuring:** The Astronauts and The Routers.
**Songs include:** *Surf Party*, *White Water*, *Crack Up*, *Glory Wave* and *If I Were An Artist*.
Three Phoenix girls take a vacation on Malibu Beach and find romance with surfers Vinton and Miller. While one of the girls Terry (Morrow) also attempts to track down her beachnik brother. A lack lustre affair that is only helped by the real surf action and a cameo by The Astronauts.

**8. Ride The Wild Surf** (1964)
**Directed by:** Don Taylor.
**Cast:** Fabian, Shelley Fabares, Tab Hunter, Peter Brown, Barbara Eden, Jim Mitchum, Susan Hart and Anthony Hart.
**Featuring:** Jan and Dean (soundtrack only)
**Songs include:** *Ride The Wild Surf*.
Fabian becomes a champion surfer when he travels to Oahu, Hawaii with his two buddies Hunter and Brown. He also finds time to romance the lovely Shelley while Robert Mitchum's son Jim puts in a showey performance as Eskimo. Add to this the Wilson/ Berry/Christian title song and Don Taylor's fine direction, Ride The Wild Surf rates as one of the best movies of the whole genre.

**9. The Girls On The Beach** (1965)
**Directed by:** William M. Whitney
**Cast:** Lana Wood, Martin West, Noreen Corcoran and Peter Brooks.
**Featuring:** The Beach Boys, The Crickets and Lesley Gore.
**Songs include:** *The Girls On The Beach, The Lonely Sea, Little Honda, La Bamba, Leave Me Alone, It's Gotta Be You* and *I Don't Want to Be A Loser.*

Three coeds spend the summer at a sorority beach house which badly needs funds to pay its mortgage. They get conned by a couple of local beach boys into believing The Beatles will do a charity concert for them. The Beach Boys rise above the almost insulting plot and perform their three songs with their heads held high. While the girls end up impersonating the Fab Four.

**10. Pajama Party** (1964)
**Directed by:** Don Weis
**Cast:** Annette Funicello, Tommy Kirk, Harvey Lembeck, Buster Keaton, Elsa Lancaster, Jody McCrea, Donna Loren, Candy Johnson, Bobbi Shaw, Jesse White, Dorothy Lamour and Ben Lessy.
**Featuring:** The Nooney Rickett Four.
**Songs include:** *Pajama Party, Beach Ball, It's That Kind of Day, There Has To Be A Reason, Where Did I Go Wrong, Among The Young* and *Stuffed Animal.*
Pajama Party introduced a new element into the routine AIP beach movie . . Sci-fi. Teenage Martian (Kirk) lands on Earth with a plan to invade. But after meeting Annette changes his mind. Eric Von Zipper (Lembeck) turns up as a motor-cycle cop while poor Buster Keaton portrays Chief Rotten Eagle . . . he should have known better. AIP carried on with this spin-off series via *The Ghost In The Invisible Bikini* (1966) and *Dr. Goldfoot and The Bikini Machine* but by that time the beach was dead.

# Folk City:
# *It Ain't Me Babe*

*I feel so sad each time, I look out there and find*
*My Woodies outside, covered in snow — no place to go now*

*New York A Lonely Town (when you're the only surfer boy)*
Anders/Poncia

**1965 found The Beatles and Bob Dylan firmly established on the consciousness of young America, add to that the escalating Vietnam War and the times were certainly-a-changing.**

**Even under such odds, there were some reluctant to give in to the new. They just had to take that one last ride . . .**

**The Surfaris and new member Ken Forssi (far left). He later joined Love. Drummer Ron Wilson recorded *As Tears Go By* under producer Brian Wilson and later scored a hit as a member of the Joy Of Cooking with Brownsville in 1971.**

By the time Murry Wilson ceased to be The Beach Boys manager, he'd already recorded his own album: *The Many Moods of Murry Wilson*. Released on Capitol Records, the sleeve notes read: 'This album is a first! Because it features Murry Wilson — songwriter! Until this time, the public has known Murry Wilson only as father and initial personal manager — recording director of the world famous Beach Boys. The man who rocketed them into a phenomenal career.

Now, it's Murry Wilson's turn! You will hear a side of Murry that only his family and close friends are aware of — the songwriter with a flair of melodic structure! And you'll also hear a fantastic mixture of sounds uncommon to most recordings.' While Murry added: 'The music business has been good to the entire Wilson family' — 'And, this album, which has been mixed as emotionally as possible, retaining color, shading and warmth, is humbly offered to the public.'

Unfortunately for Murry, the vast record buying public decided to ignore his offer and the album sank with out as much as a ripple.

Realizing his own limitations, Murry decided to look for a new Beach Boys to handle, and he soon found them via his son Carl. For Carl introduced his dad to eighteen year old Rick Henn, a drummer from Westwood. Henn also composed his own songs and had a voice similar to that of the Four Seasons' Frankie Valli.

With Henn as a nucleus it was just a simple matter of finding the right musicians and The Sunrays were born.

The final quintet included three ex-members of The Snowmen; lead guitarist Eddie Medora, rhythm guitarist Byron Case and pianist Marty Di Giovanni.

The Snowmen's only claim to fame was the local hit *Ski Storm* released on the Challenge label in '63. Finally, bass player Vince Hozier was added to the line-up.

Wilson set-up a recording deal with Tower Records and the group's debut single *I Live For The Sun* was released in the summer of '65. Produced by Murry and written by Rick; *I Live For the Sun* quickly climbed into the top fifty. The song was also a hit for Vanity Fare in the UK.

They followed *I Live For The Sun* with a

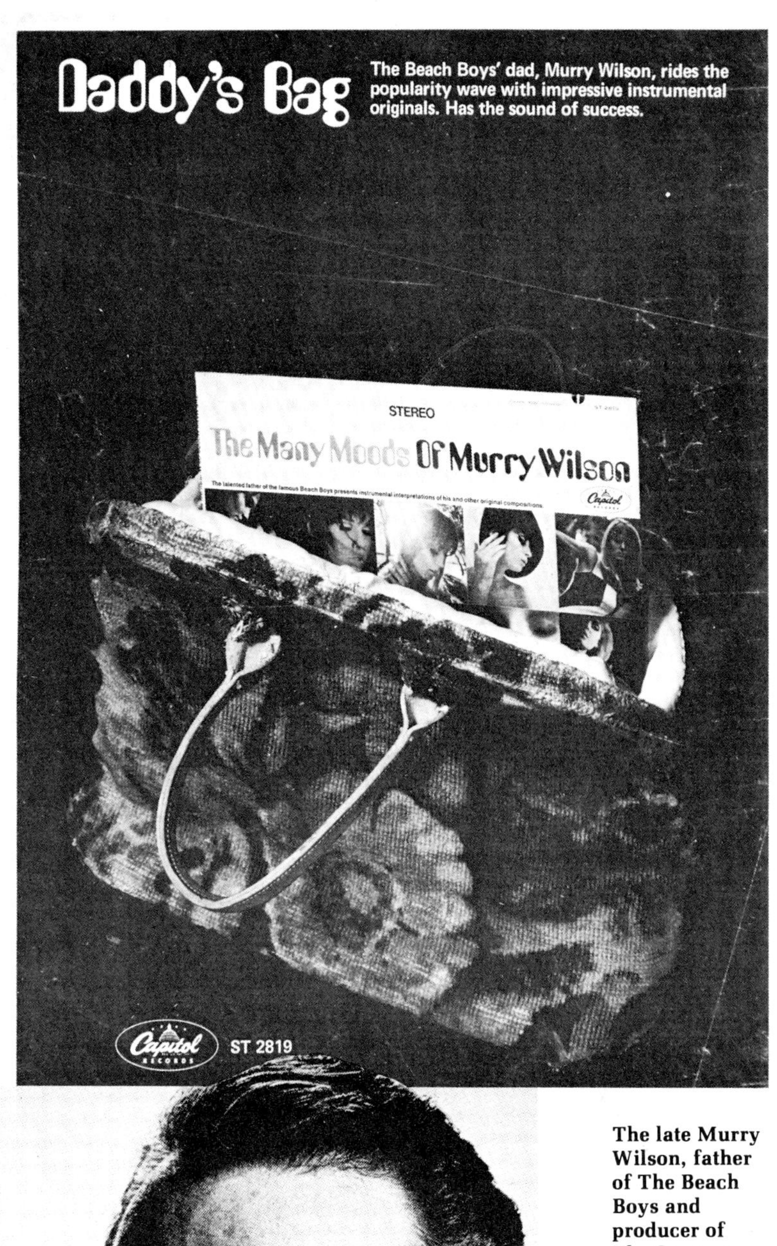

The late Murry Wilson, father of The Beach Boys and producer of The Sunrays.

**Above: The Sunrays L/R Marty, Rick, Byron, Eddie and Vince. Opposite: The Fantastic Baggies L/R Drummer Bob Myman, Phil, Steve and Jerry Cargman.**

couple of hot rod songs *Car Party* and *Outta Gas* without the same success. Their second and biggest hit *Andrea* (another Henn original), found them very much in the Four Seasons territory and it eventually peaked at number forty-one. *Andrea* also became the title of their first album. Produced by Murry Wilson and Don Ralke (who helped give Jan and Arnie their first hit), apart from including *I Live For The Sun* it was on the whole a very Four Season's sounding set especially on tracks such as *I Look Baby — I Can't See* and *You Don't Phase Me*. Murry Wilson contributed *Bye Baby Bye* while the country sounding *Still* was chosen as The Sunray's final hit single.

Over on the East Coast, keeping the flame alive The Tradwinds climbed into the top thirty with *New Yorks A Lonely Town*. The song perfectly captured the frustration of living in New York City when surfing was all the rage in California:

*My folks moved to New York from California*
*I should have listened what my buddy said,*
*I warn you.*

The press release that accompanied the disc described The Tradewinds as a 'four strong group from Providence' when they were in fact the studio creation of Pete Anders and Vinnie Poncia (who also penned the song). The disc was released in January '65 and quickly rose into the top thirty. Sadly, it was The Tradewinds only surf release although the flip-side *Club Seventeen* also sounded very surf-like.

However, the most prolific surf songwriting duo who went about masquarading as a group were Phil Sloan and Steve Barri. Although their most famous alias was The Fantastic Baggys, they also recorded surf music as The Lifeguards, Willie and The Wheels, The Rincon Surfside Band, and The Rally Packs.

As The Lifeguards, they released *Swimtime U.S.A.* on Frank Sinatra's Reprise label in April '64. Four months later they made their debut as The Fantastic Baggy singing the background parts and supplying songs for Jan and Dean's *Ride The Wild Surf* album. Phillip (Flip) Sloan was born in New York, but moved to LA with his family in his early teens. Months later at the age of fourteen he made his debut disc for the R&B Alladin label. Sloan: 'I auditioned singing Little Richard, Thurston Harris songs. It was a black label. 'Bumps' Blackwell (co-writer of many Little Richard hits) produced me on a song I wrote.'

The disc — *All I Want is Loving* failed to make a chart placing, and Phil dropped out for a year to concentrate on his schooling. He soon returned to the record business via The Mart Label.

While Phil was producing such unforgetables as *If You Believe In Me* and *She's My Girl* for Mart, Steve Barri was working in a record store over in Fairfax. In his sparetime he started writing his own songs The Nortones picked-up his *Susie Jones* while he got himself a record deal with the local Rona label in '61.

He didn't gain much success until he teamed up with ex-Teddybear Carol Connors and her sister Cheryl, and as The Storytellers, released their first disc *When Two People*. The record was originally released on the mini Ramark label, but, was soon picked-up by entrepreneur Lou Adler for Dimension Records. Although the disc failed to make the grade it was to mark the start of a successful career with Phil under the management of Adler.

Sloan: 'I finally got an interview with Lou Adler. He wouldn't sign me, but he said I could come up every day after school and write. Barri had a record which was bought as a master by Adler (probably *When Two People* for Dimension). He was into singing and had no need to hook up with an unknown kid songwriter. I was getting a few songs published up there on my own. Anyway, Steve's record bombed, so he was no longer needed. I was in the piano room and he walked in. Adler said, 'I'd like the two of you to try writing together.' So I played him about ten songs, one of which was *Unless You Care* and part of another, *Kick That Little Foot, Sally Ann.*

Barrie got excited and said "Okay". Then I said, "Well, what have you got?" He played me some stuff on the ukulele.'

Adler soon had them turning out songs for Jan and Dean, while The Rip Chords and Bruce and Terry covered *This Little Woody, Surfin' Craze* and *Summer Mean Fun* among others. The latter tracks were also featured on The Fantastic Baggy's *Tell 'Em I'm Surfin'* album. Released on Imperial in late '64, the album also featured sleeve notes by Lou Adler: 'As in the history of the United States, development seems to go from East to West, for in the last two years the West Coast Sound or, as it is sometimes called, the Surfin' Sound, has busted wide open with such outstanding producer-writer talents as Brian Wilson (The Beach Boys) — the Daniel Boone of the West Coast Sound; Terry Melcher (The Rip Chords); and Jan Berry of Jan and Dean.

Now two more young and very talented boys join this new frontier; Phil (flip) Sloan and Steve Barri.'

One of the more interesting cuts on the album was the final track . . . Sloan and Barri's *Surfin's Back Again — Surf Impressions.* Judging by the lyrics, they must have realized their days were numbered — 'Say, boy what's the matter with your head, don't you know surfin's dead.' At the finale (*The Surf Impressions* seque) they impersonate among others Jan Berry, Brian Wilson, Lou Adler, and Terry ('Stay away from my eyes, boy') Melcher.

Phil: 'Terry would get smashed on wine and the next day he could hardly see straight. He couldn't "find his eyes." One night Jan had a party and got smashed and

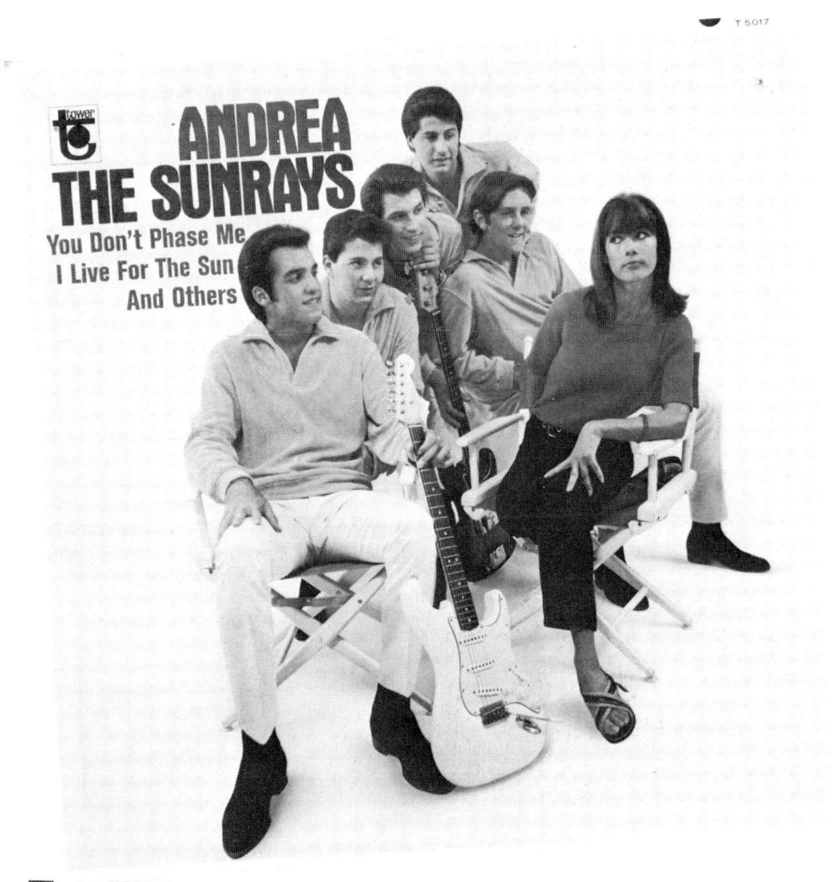




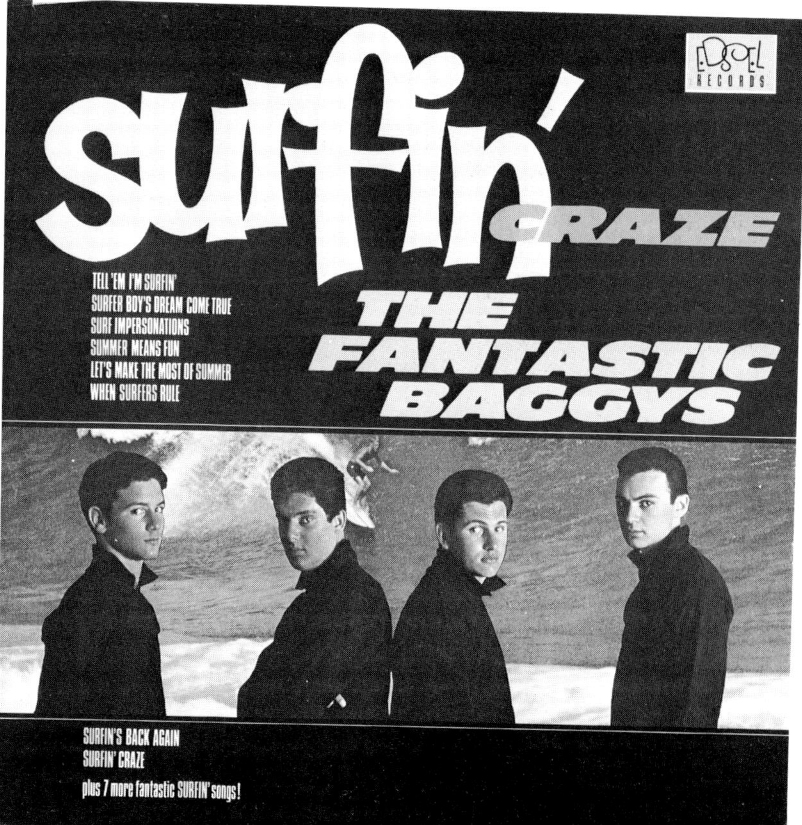

**Above: The Byrds. Chris Hillman, David Crosby, Gene Clark and Jim McGuinn performing in LA.**

was crawling on the carpet yelling, "keep away from my eyes!" Terry thought that was hysterical and repeated it for six months. I never thought anyone would hear those impersonations to begin with.'

Apart from tippling Vino, Melcher was also on the brink of discovering a new West Coast sound . . . Folk Rock. Adler meanwhile, along with Pierre Cossette and Bobby Roberts had formed Dunhill, a company specializing in production, management and publishing. But, by the spring of '65 Dunhill had become a bonafide record company in its own right.

Although their early releases found them without any real direction . . . Ritchie Weems; *Natural Born Man*, Shelley Fabares; *My Prayer* and with a reluctancy to abandon the surf genre (that after all Adler knew it so well), Willie And The Wheels; *Skateboard Craze.*

*Skateboard Craze* was at least an attempt to emulate Jan and Dean's '64 *Sidewalk Surfin'* hit — however, the disc was released in May '65 — the very month The Byrds captured the Charts with their 'Beatlelized Dylan' Melcher produced song *Mr. Tambourine Man.*

Billy James: 'They brought it all back home. *Mr. Tambourine Man* was Columbia's first number one single since Steve Lawrence's daringly double-voiced *Go Away Little Girl.* I was afraid they'd blow The Byrds since they seemed to ignore Dylan for three years — I would step out of line to tell them to push him, I would get memos back from the Vice President of Marketing saying why doesn't Dylan save his best material for himself.
But they sure sold a lot of Byrds records.'

The mood of the times had suddenly sized the charts; and Melcher for the first time in his recording history became one of its foremost brand leaders.

The Byrds were formed in the Summer of '64 by Gene Clark after seeing Jim McGuinn performing Beatle songs at LA's Troubadour Club. McGuinn had also a lot of folk music behind him and had even appeared on the caberet circuit, backing Bobby Darin. With the arrival of David Crosby they started calling themselves The Jet Set.

Then the guitar orientated trio was joined by bass player Chris Hillman, drummer Mike Clarke and manager Jim Dickson who soon acquired (for them) a one record and option deal with Electra Records.

The Beatlish single *Please Let Me Love You* was released in the Autumn of '64, under the name of The Beefeaters . . .

Jac Holzman (president of Electra): 'I plead guilty . . . but there had been such a run of British groups.'

The record failed, the option dropped and the group changed their name to The Byrds and booked into LA's World Pacific Studios under Dickson's guidance to cut new demos.

The resulting tracks (later released as the album *Preflyte*), featured ten original songs plus a cover of Dylan's *Mr. Tambourine Man.* McGuinn: 'In the spectrum of music at the time . . . I saw this gap, with Dylan and The Beatles leaning towards each other in concept. That's where we aimed.'

Their sound fell within hearing distance of Terry Melcher, he was keen on the musical concept, but insisted on the tried and tested session crew of Campbell, Blaine, Leon Russell and Larry Knetchel (to complement the group's vocal arrangement). Only McGuinn's twelve-string

**Above: One-step above the master . . . Bobby Dylan and The Byrds. Left: The multi-talented producer extraordinaire Terry Melcher.**

Rickenbacker remained from the original instrumental track. It worked! Mr Tambourine Man became number one in the nation and the surfin' Fender guitar sound took a temporary back seat to the jingle-janglish Rickenbacker. Overnight, the new sound swept Surfin' way down the Swanee and suddenly there was a brand new direction to follow. By the time The Byrds secured their second number one hit single, *Turn, Turn, Turn* the West Coast record industry was alive with folk-rockers.

The Crossfires included a folk spot in their act, dubbed The Crosswind Singers (they were now becoming more of a vocal outfit).

KRLA disc jockey Rebb Foster who also owned the Revelaire Club at Redondo Beach became their manager in early '65 . . . And, the Crossfires soon became the club's house band. It was while appearing at the club Ted Feigin of the newly formed White Whale Records company caught their new folk-rock act and signed them to the label.

There was only one hitch, Feigin didn't like their name and between him and Foster came up with a new one The Turtles. Mark Volman: 'He (Rebb Foster) would've spelled it with a "Y" if he could.'



**The Turtles, left to right: Howard Kaylan, Mark Volman, Jim Pons, John Seiter and Al Nichol.**

Under their new name and new sound, the group released Dylan's *It Ain't Me Babe* and by August '65 it was firmly established in the top ten.

Although still committed to several new surf releases (including The Rincon Surfside Band's *Surfing Songbook* album), Sloan and Barri were quick to latch on to the new Californian sound. Phil, who was by now going under the name PF Sloan released the Dylan-esque *The Sins of The Family* on Dunhill in the summer of '65 while he also contributed songs to other Dunhill folk rock acts including *Eve of Destruction* for Barry McGuire and *You Baby* for The Mamas & Papas.

Sloan: 'I was so busy then. I had the candle lit both ends. I was going from The Turtle's sessions to the McGuire sessions to The Mamas & Papas sessions to the Jan and Dean sessions to the Grass Roots' sessions to the Fantastic Baggy's sessions to my own sessions. Then, as a side gig, I was the guitar player on some beer commercials and playing guitar on other people's recording dates all over the city. I was also writing by myself and writing with Steve and producing by myself. There had to have been a split personality, because I couldn't be in that many places at one time. I was twenty years old!

I loved Dylan, listened to his first album for six months. I remember the first four songs I wrote away from Barri one night. They were *Eve of Destruction, The Sins of The Family, This Mornin'* and *Take Me For What I'm Worth.* No one at Dunhill liked these songs except Adler.'

Ex-New Christy Minstrel, McGuire took the *Eve of Destruction* protest song, to the number one position; While the UK Searchers trailed in the hot hundred with *Take Mc For What I'm Worth.* Phil Sloan: 'I was thrilled by The Searchers recording of that song. You see, I was getting most of my songs recorded by that small family (The Turtles, Barry McGuire, Shelley Fabares, Johnny Rivers and Jan and Dean). The Searchers had no connection with them. I never sent it to them. The record had imagination . . . the guitars and all. I really enjoyed it.'

It's widely considered that The Searchers in fact were the original folk rockers. This becomes clear when listening to the jingle-jangle Rickenbacker guitar and close harmonies of their '64 hit *Needles and Pins*. The same overall sound was used to great effect on The Byrds, *I'll Feel A Whole Lot Better* (from their *Mr. Tambourine Man* album — produced by Terry Melcher), and The Surfaris' *Hey Joe (Where are You Going)*. The Surfaris *Hey Joe* just fell short of the top hundred but, many fans were disappointed when it was not included on their *It Ain't Me Babe* album. Gary Usher's first venture into the Folk Rock genre.

Released in November '65, *It Ain't Me Babe* was a typical Surfaris album. Produced by Usher and his famed session crew, with the occasional help from the odd Surfari (mainly Ron Wilson). The album featured an array of current hits including Dylan's *Like A Rolling Stone, All I Really Want To Do* and the title song.

The front sleeve featured the group including lead guitarist Jim Fuller with his recently acquired Rickenbacker (he soon left as Pat Connolly — "in disgust") and new bass-player Ken Forssi. The sleeve notes were written by their newly acquired manager Dick Martinek: 'Within a relatively short period of two years, that quintet of talented performers, The Surfaris have played and sung their way into the hearts of youngsters both in America and abroad.

While the majority of their hit recordings have been their own compositions, several of their best-selling albums, such as *Hit City '65* have contained a number of songs originally popularized by other artists.

Martinek went on to explain how he was propositioned by two Decca Records executives to manage The Surfaris. 'For once, Lady Luck was on my side.' He continued: 'I wondered what was wrong — where was the catch?'

The catch was . . . After the failure of the album *It Ain't Me Babe* and the single *Hey Joe* to make the charts, Decca Records didn't renew their contract.

Ken Forssi soon split (taking with him the arrangement of *Hey Joe*), and joined Arthur Lee's Love — who soon recorded the song. It featured on their debut album *Love*. Released in March '66 the album produced one top fifty hit Bacharach and David's *Little Red Book* (originally recorded by Manfred Mann for the film *What's New*

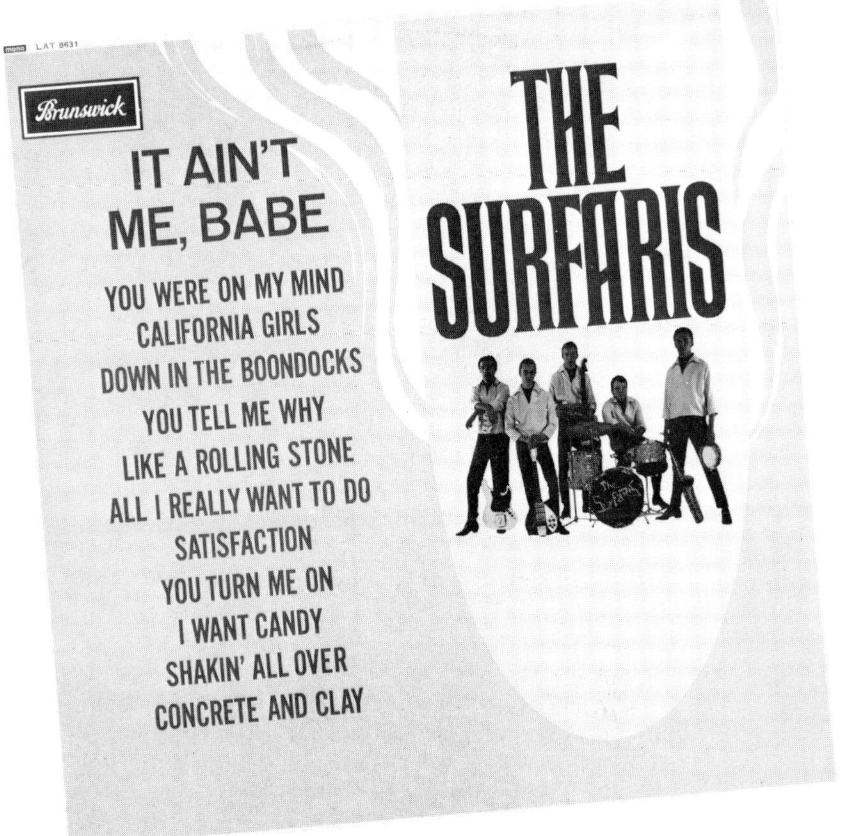


**The final Surfaris album.**



*Pussycat* (1965). Love, gained their biggest hit, with *Seven And Seven* in the summer of '66. While The Surfaris with their new line-up including Ron Wilson, Jim Pash (now, lead guitarist), Steve Johnson; rhythm guitar and a new bassist Jack Oldham — thanks to Martinek found themselves back at Dot Records.

For their new outing on Dot, the single *Showbiz* (a Ron Wilson original reminiscent of The Byrds *So You Want To Be A Rock 'N' Roll Star*) coupled with Jack Oldham's *Chicago Green* was produced by J.J. Cale — it also failed to gain a chart entry. Their second chart assault; Pash and Johnson's Search (produced by Dick Martinek), was another flop but, alas the disc found Ron Wilson missing from the line-up. There were plans for a new Surfaris album, but after the departure of the last remaining original member Jim Pash, the project was scrapped.

Back at Dunhill, where the musical policy became completely hooked on Folk Rock . . . thanks to the advice of hit-maker Barry McGuire, Adler signed The Mamas and The Papas. Original folkies from New

**The Dunhill hopefuls The Mamas & Papas.**

**Left to right: Denny Doherty, Cass Elliot, Michelle and John Phillips.**



York's Greenwich Village Scene, The Mamas & Papas consisted of John Phillips, Cass Elliot, Denny Doherty and Michelle (Gillian) Phillips. Adler, soon took them into the studio along with the regular LA session crew — Blaine, Campbell etc and turned out a string of hits, including *California Dreamin'*, *Monday, Monday*, *I Saw Her Again* and *Creeque Alley*.

The Mamas & The Papas like The Byrds are a different (complete) story ... Returning to the original surf crowd, Dick Dale had an attempt at the new contemporary sound with the old Kingston Trio's classic *Greenback Dollar* (funny how it seems — written by Barry McGuire) while, he also tipped his hat at the master by including Dylan's *Blowin' In The Wind* on his '65 *Rock Out* album. The Beach Boys in their turn (probably thanks to original folkie Al Jardine) covered Dylan's *The Times They Are A Changin'* but also gained a massive hit with their arrangement of the folk standard *Sloop John B*. Jan and Dean also fell in-line and released the album *Folk 'N' Roll* including such folk rock hits as *It Ain't Me Babe* and *Turn, Turn, Turn* plus, Jan's own reworking of *Surf City* . . . entitled of course; *Folk City*.

By Chart standards the original surfers gained little in the new idiom. Although, in fairness, The Beach Boys were taking their own path as they always did. It was at least new ground for Terry Melcher and Gary Usher. Melcher continued off and on recording The Byrds while Usher produced two of the groups most outstanding albums; *The Notorious Byrd Brothers* and *Sweetheart Of The Rodeo*.

However, the times were changing faster than ever and California soon had a new rock capitol . . . San Francisco. The Byrds; Gene Clark: 'I like long hair but those cats in San Francisco! It's going too far!'

...a big new single for a big new year!

Released by trade demand
from their current hit LP
"FOLK 'N ROLL" · LST-7431/LRP-3431

Produced by Jan Berry
for Screen Gems, Inc.

# Out Of The Sandbox & Into The Fire: *The Beach Boys' Golden Days*

*Surf's Up, aboard a tidal wave*
*Come about hard and join the young*
*And often spring you gave.*

*Surf's Up*—Brian Wilson—Van Dyke Parks

**1964 had been a great artistic and commercial success in The Beach Boys story. They were for the most part about the only US group to stand up to the English invasion while keeping their image and musical identity intact.**

However, 1965 was to herald the start of what was to become known as the sixties rock revolution. It was a year that witnessed The Beatles' *Yesterday* and *Rubber Soul*, Dylan's *Like A Rolling Stone* and *Bringing It All Back Home*, The Stones' *(I Can't Get No) Satisfaction*, and making their chart debuts Simon and Garfunkel, The Byrds, The Lovin' Spoonful, Sonny and Cher and The Mamas and The Papas among many others.

The Beach Boys kicked off the year with another neo-Spector production *Do You Wanna Dance*, Brian's reworking of the Bobby Freeman rocker. Its flip-side was even more interesting and featured the Brian Wilson original *Please Let Me Wonder*, a yearning ballad that in some ways offered a taster in the style of the *Pet Sounds* album that would surface a year later.

**About to break new ground.**
**The Beach Boys**
**Left to right: Mike Love, Carl Wilson, Al Jardine, Dennis Wilson and big brother Brian.**

Now Brian had retired from the road, his production genius was beginning to fully flower. The rest of the group still felt uneasy about performing without the chief. Brian: 'I told them I foresee a beautiful future for The Beach Boys' group but the only way we could achieve it was if they did their job and I did mine. They would have to get a replacement for me . . . I didn't say "they". I said "we" because it isn't they and me, it's us.'

The album's sleeve was also a new departure — gone were the trappings of the surf and auto culture — just a straight line-up pic of the group in their new woollies. But its most important feature was the high level of Brian's songwriting and producing talent. Brian Wilson: 'Six months ago, I bought a new house up in Beverly Hills . . . I arranged the house so I had a big room full of music and atmosphere, and I started to plan the new direction of the group . . . I wanted to move ahead in sounds and melodies and moods. For months, I plotted and planned. For a month or two I sat either at a huge Spanish table looking out over the hills, just thinking, or at the piano playing "feels". Feels, are muscial ideas, riffs; bridges, fragments of themes. A phrase here and there.

This method of songwriting had ambitious aims. I wanted to write a song containing more than one level. Eventually, I would like to see longer singles . . . so that the song can be more meaningful . . . A song can, for instance, have movements, in the same way as a classical concerto, only capsulized.'



The first musician they chose to fill in for Brian was Glen Campbell, a natural choice as Glen had appeared on practically all their records since '63. Campbell: 'I usually played rhythm on their sessions . . . When it came to being one of The Beach Boys, they called me. They said, "We got a gig in Dallas day after tomorrow. You want to play with us?" "You mean open the show for you?" I asked. "No, Brian's sick and can't make it. We need somebody to play bass and sing the high parts." "Yeah, sure." I didn't know all the lyrics. It was fun — an experience.'

While Glen was touring with the group Brian was putting finishing touches to their new album *The Beach Boys Today*. The album was split into two very different moods; side one was very much for dancing . . . *Do You Wanna Dance, Good To My Baby, Dance, Dance, Dance* and the original *Help Me Rhonda* — complete with harmonica and fade outs, while it also included *When I Grow Up* and *Don't Hurt My Little Sister*. Side two was for romancing; *Please Let Me Wonder, Kiss Me Baby* and the almost overlooked classic *She Knows Me Too Well* were included in the programme.

**Right: Brian's first replacement. The brilliant Glen Campbell.**

Around this time Brian and Phil Spector did a few sessions together, Brian even played piano on Spector's version of his *Don't Hurt My Little Sister*. Sadly, Spector never released the disc. Brian once recalled the sessions: 'I was able to perceive very much more than he thought I could. I was a little more alert . . . I basically knew all that was to be known about that (wall of sound) simply by listening, using my ears.'

Gary Usher cut *Don't Hurt My Little Sister* with his usual crew plus Ron Wilson singing lead and released it as a Surfaris single. However, it wasn't his first choice. Al Jardine: 'It was *Rhonda* I had difficulty with . . . It was the second song I sang lead on. I was used to singing background. It was a whole different thing . . . quite complex . . .

It seems quite simple now but it's something called timing meter and rhythm. It was a matter of getting your mind-body concentration together . . . Finally it came together real well. The way we cut the first version was different from the way we sang the second . . . When Gary Usher decided he might want to cover it, we decided to get a version out first. So Brian raced in and said, "Let's do it again".'

It was definitely the right decision for their new updated version stormed the charts giving them their second number one hit single. Al must have been a proud man.

Back on the road, Glen Campbell was doing a fine job filling in for Brian. Audree Wilson: 'Glen is tall, and his hair is lighter than Brian's, but a lot of kids in the audience would think he was Brian. They'd yell "Brian! Brian!" The Beach Boys asked Glen to join permanently, but after six months Campbell decided to follow a solo career. Glen Campbell: 'If the Beach Boys did something, then I did it. And I didn't like that at all . . . I'm probably too much of an individual.'

After he gave the group his decision, Mike Love called Bruce Johnston and asked him if he knew of a bass player who could fill in on a forthcoming tour. Bruce couldn't think of anyone available and offered his services.

The Beach Boys accepted and on 9th April, '65 at the Wilminton, Delaware concert, Bruce became the eighth official group member. Johnston: 'So Brian left the road, initially Glen Campbell filled in, and in April '65 I got a call to take his place. I jumped on to a plane to New Orleans, squeezed into a pair of Al Jardine's pants that were three sizes too small and four inches too short and five hours later I was on stage singing *Surfin' U.S.A.*, and that's how I joined The Beach Boys.'

**New boy, Bruce Johnston is recruited.**

Bruce's first recording session with the group turned out to be their new single *California Girls*. Bruce: 'Brian just said "Here, sing a part" and I sang a part and it worked.' It certainly did — *California Girls* with its unmistakable keyboard intro and sunny harmonies went top three in July.

Brian: 'It kind of represents California living. It's so centered on California. It has to do with my interest in girls. There's nothing greater than a girl . . . Well, a kid, your daughter, but that's a girl too. It reflects my philosophy. It's kind of a high point of Mike Love's career . . . It features Mike Love as a great rock-and-roll singer . . . not to mention that it has some good harmony, plus a good background track. If you listen, you'll hear that the instruments are playing really nice. We had a lot of musicians supporting the Beach Boys, including a lot of Phil Spector's musicians.'

Brian's then regular session musicians included Glen Campbell, Tommy Tedesco, Ray Pohlman, Barney Kessel and Jerry Cole on guitars; Steve Douglas, Roy Caton, Jay Migliori and Lou Blackburn — horns; Lyle Ritz, Julius Wechler and Carol Kaye — bass; Leon Russell, Don Randi and Al De Lory — piano; Carl Fortina and Frank Marocco — accordion; Tommy Morgan — harmonica; and Hal Blaine — percussion. *California Girls* was released to coincide with the release of the group's new album *Summer Days And Summer Nights*.

On the whole, the album had a great California good time feel and apart from Brian's continued musical experiments that reached a new zenith on *Let Him Run Wild* and *You're So Good To Me*, the other Beach Boys were spotlighted throughout the rest of the album.

Mike never sounded better than on his lead vocal outings that included (the already mentioned) *California Girls*, *The Girl From New York City* and *Amusement Parks U.S.A.* Brian: 'You should have seen Mike diggin' his own voice when we played back *The Girl From New York City* in the studio last week. He was movin' and groovin' like he used to in the locker room at Dorsey High.'

Carl got his big chance on *Girl Don't Tell Me*, while Al sang lead on Brian's reworking of Spector's *Then I Kissed Her* — that later became a chart topper in the UK and the group completed side two with an acapella . . . *And Your Dream Comes True*.

It seems their dreams had come true, *Summer Days And Summer Nights* went gold, reaching the number two position in the album charts.

The album sleeve also rates as one of the most unusual in the group's career, for the front cover featured only four Beach Boys. Al: 'I missed the boat on this album cover. The very day the pictures were taken I had to spend in bed with a flu bug instead of on a yacht with the photographer.'

Judging by a pic used on the 80's *Rarities* album, Bruce was at the photo session but, for contractual reasons (Bruce was still officially signed to Columbia), he had to remain a 'Phantom Beach Boy.'

The Beach Boys' fourth single of '65, *The Little Girl I Once Knew*, became their least commercial and stalled at number twenty. The song was, in fact, one of Brian's most adventurous to date — full of tempo changes and complete stops. Brian: 'Somebody said, "Let's take a four-beat pause." I said, "fine."'

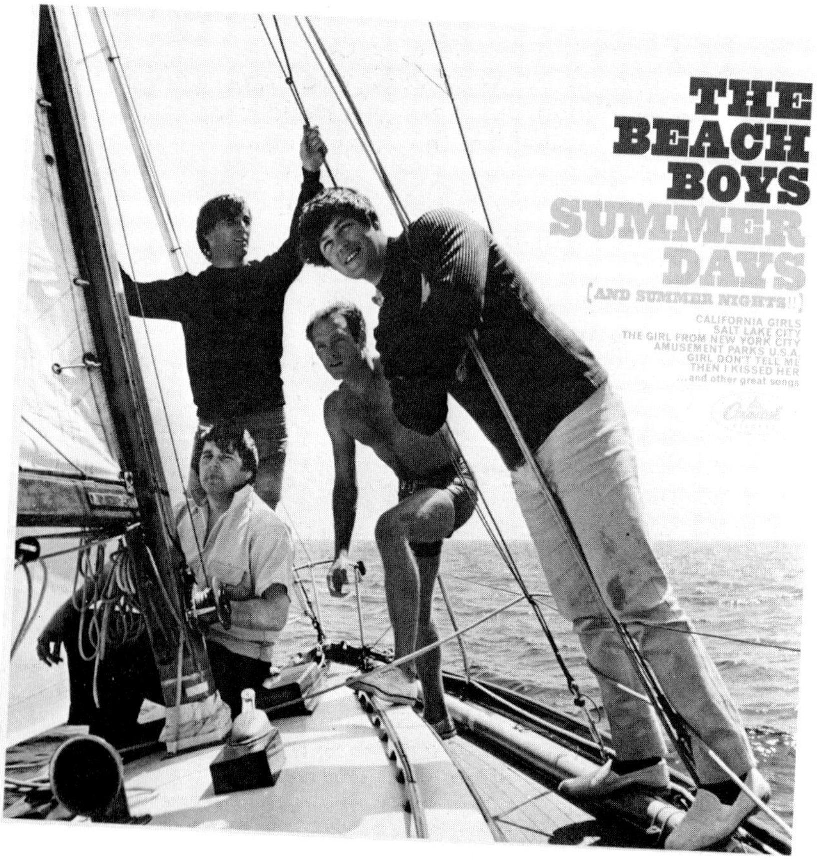

The single's lack of success was just a minor setback, for Brian had already envisaged a concept album that would set the record straight, thereby establishing the group as one of the leaders in rock music. But, he needed time to develop his ideas and time was one thing Capitol Records wouldn't give him. Nick Venet: 'They pressured him into doing an album every twenty-four hours.' To satisfy the company's demand, Brian decided to pull out a quickie, just to keep them off his back. He decided on a live album, but not a concert . . . a *Beach Boys Party*. Chuck Britz: 'We did it at Studio Two and we had a kind of PA deal and everybody just sat down and started playing and singing. Everybody was joining in as they walked into the studio. Diane and Marilyn were there, Carl and his wife-to-be (they weren't married at the time). Dean, Phil Sloan, Jan Berry. There was none of that animosity between groups. People would just walk in and have a good time. It was all done live. In that day and age a lot of things just happened. We did a lot of gimmick things. We did the bottle popping — a lot of things for experimental purposes.'

Marilyn remembered that the album started at a party at Mike's house, and they just moved it into the studio. A reporter from *Teen Set* was at one of the sessions: 'Dennis Wilson put in an appearance, but he was suffering from bronchitis (caused by skin-diving with a bad cold) and was sent home. Hal Blaine did drum duty for the group. Mike Love brought in four suits which he had ordered from New York and began trying them on, using one of the microphones for a coat rack . . .

By now it was 7 pm and the drummer was scheduled to leave at 8. Panic. They began running through three songs — *Hully Gully*, *I Should Have Known Better* and *Tell Me Why* . . . they had obviously been over the songs during the previous session; everyone seemed to know the timing. It was only a question of getting the right balance of voices and instruments.

Rather than take one song at a time, Brian chose to go through all three in a row for a rough idea. They made it by eight, at which time they adjourned to the control room to listen to the playback.' The album's overall sound was heavily acoustic with solid vocal harmonies and the bass, bongos and tambourines keeping the backbeat, it worked perfectly. The Beach Boys had created a mini masterpiece without the aid of sophisticated strings and other exotic instruments. Albeit refined in the studio, the album had a definite homemade appeal.

Apart from their easy-going covers of The Beatles' *I Should Have Known Better* and *Tell Me Why*, Dennis was given the vocal spotlight on *You've Got To Hide Your Love Away*. They also acknowledged Dylan when Al sang *The Times They Are A-Changin'*, and sent themselves up on *I Get Around* and *Little Deuce Coupe*.

Brian and Mike sang The Everly Brothers' *Devoted To You* in original fashion, while the whole crowd joined in on the chorus of perhaps the stand-out track: *There's No Other*. With a few fillers such

as *Papa-Omm-Mow-Mow*, *Alley Oop* and *Mountain of Love* they were stuck for a final song. Dean Torrence: 'The Beach Boys were down the hall in the next studio cutting the *Beach Boys Party* album. I walked into the Beach Boys session or — oops, should I say party (hope I didn't spoil any illusions about a swinging party at the Wilsons' house) and they were all sitting around trying to think of another song to do. So they asked me what I wanted to sing. I said *Barbara Ann* for what reason I don't remember.'

Dean sang along with the group and it became the perfect finale for the album. The album sleeve featured party and beach pics of Brian and Marilyn, Carl and Annie, Dennis and girlfriend, Al and Lynda and Mike but still no sign of Bruce.

Released in November, *The Beach Boys Party* rose to number six in the album charts. Capitol Records (without The Beach Boys' knowledge) put out *Barbara Ann* as a single and it eventually peaked at number two in January '66.

The success of both the album and single

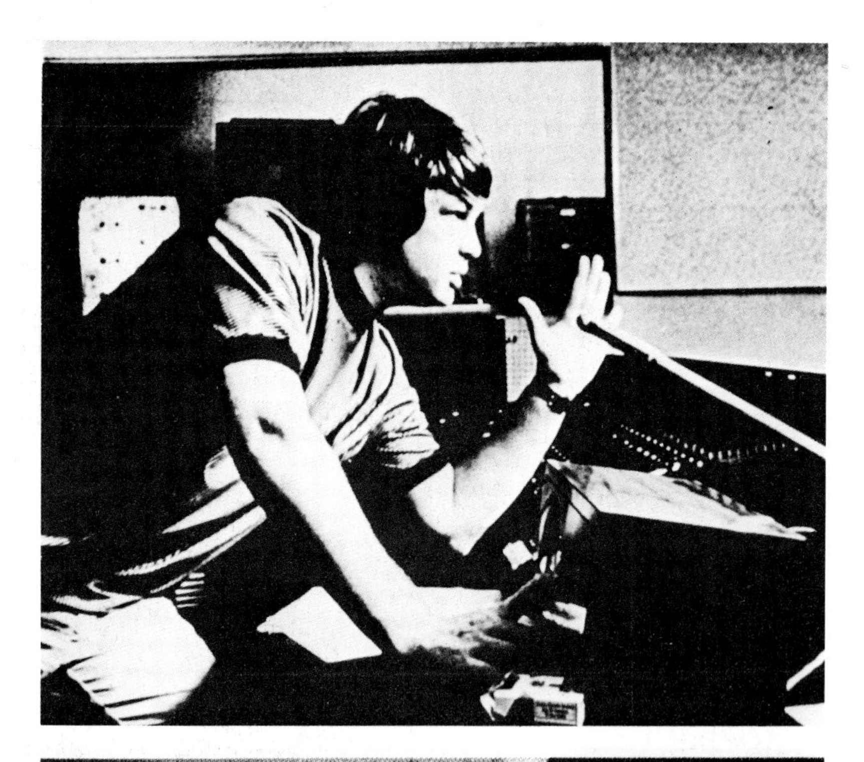

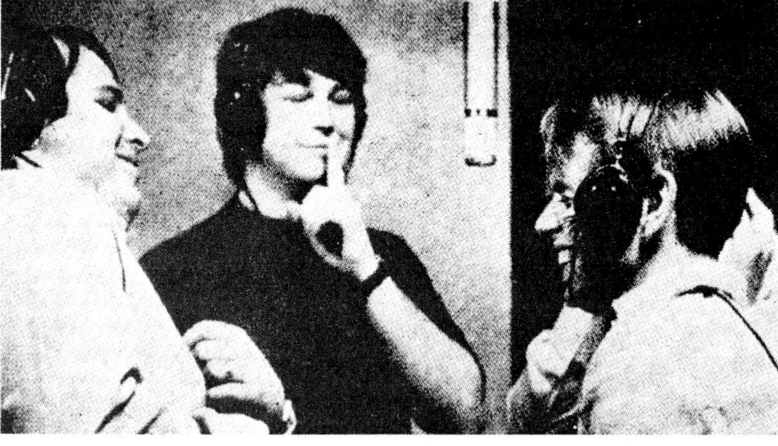



**Above: Brian at his best . . . in the studio.**

**Far right: The touring Beach Boys hear the news that their striped shirts are soon to be replaced.**

gave Brian a little breathing space to concentrate on the album that was to become his personal best. Wilson seemed to be locked into a competition with The Beatles' *Rubber Soul* album and he began preparing *Pet Sounds*. His new inspiration at the time had only produced two new unfinished tracks . . . a new arrangement of the traditional folk song *Sloop John B* complete with piccolos and flutes, and a new Brian Wilson composition, *In My Childhood*. Al had suggested covering *Sloop John B* during the *All Summer Long* sessions two years earlier. The original song came from Al's folk music background and was originally published in a collection by the American folk song specialist Carl Sandburg. *John B* originates from the West Indies where the historic Sloop lies embedded in the sand at Governor's Harbour, Nassau. Al: 'I played some chords. He came back and arranged an entire symphony around it.'

Brian was unhappy with the finished lyric of *In My Childhood* and called in a new collaborator, Tony Asher, to supply new lyrics . . . It eventually surfaced on the album as *You Still Believe In Me*.

Asher was, at the time, an advertising copywriter and had written several successful jingles, and it was while at a recording studio working on one of them, that he was introduced to Brian. Asher: 'I was really just interested in a regular income. Security y'know. I'm a pretty conservative guy.'

Although Brian came up with all the ideas for the album, he doubted his own ability to pull off the lyrics and felt Asher to be sympathic to his new direction. Brian: 'I've always been insecure about my lyrics. I always felt that what I wanted to say was never imparted in my lyrics . . . that the message just wasn't there.'

Asher finally contributed lyrics to another seven songs that appeared on *Pet Sounds*, including *Wouldn't It Be Nice, God Only Knows, Caroline No, That's Not Me, Don't Talk (put your head on my shoulder), Here Today* and *I Just Wasn't Made For These Times*. Asher: 'It's fair to say that the general tenor of the lyrics was always his and the actual choice of words was usually mine. I was really just his interpreter.' While Brian and Tony had been working on *Pet Sounds*, The Beach Boys had been touring Japan, and on their return Brian played them the basic tracks. On first hearing, Mike was less than enthused. Love: 'Well, It sure sounds different to the old stuff.' However, he soon came around and supplied the lyrics for *I'm Waiting For The Day*.

Asher: 'Well I always thought Al Jardine was a kind of underrated force in the band. I mean, I felt he was genuinely impressed by some of the music we were making. He'd take me aside sometimes and tell me how good it was.

Brian had a bigger problem with *Hang On To Your Ego*, a song he'd written with ex-Beach Boys roadie Terry Sachen, for the group rebelled and refused to participate on a song with a title like that. So Brian was forced to change it — the song eventually surfaced as *I Know There's An Answer*.

Brian was especially pleased with *Caroline No*, and decided to put it out as a solo single. Bruce Johnston: 'That song was directly about Brian himself and the death of a quality within him that was so vital — his innocence. He knows it too.'

Murry Wilson handled the final mix on the single, and speeded up the track so the original key of G became the key of A, making Brian sound younger.

Derek Taylor: 'Murry was always out of his depth. There was no malice in him whatsoever, mind. He was just a hot-shot from the suburbs.'

All this pressure was beginning to tell on Brian, he was also into heavy drugs and doing far-out things . . . such as building a sandbox in his living room where he could sit at his piano and compose.

*Caroline No*, coupled with *Summer Means New Love* (an instrumental originally featured on *Summer Days And Summer Nights*), crept into the top thirty. However, *Sloop John B*, released a couple of weeks later, thundered into the top three.

The *Pet Sounds* album was released in May '66 and although it has been hailed as one of rock music's milestones, commercially it failed to live up to Capitol Records' expectations. In fact Capitol had insisted on the inclusion of the hit single *Sloop John B* to help sales. Brian was against the idea, for the song was never planned to be included on the album and in many ways upset the continuity of the album's overall concept. For apart from *Sloop John B* each song seemed to pinpoint a crisis of faith and love from the opening *Wouldn't It Be Nice* to *Caroline No* at the closing.

Brian added a non-musical coda on the end of *Caroline No* . . . the sound of a clanging train and his own dogs Banana and Louie barking. Brian: 'Remember the dogs? That was the whole idea . . . calling it *Pet Sounds* after the dogs.'

The album also featured two highly distinctive instrumentals — *Pet Sounds* and *Let's Go Away For A While* (Asher supplied lyrics for the latter but they were not used). The front cover sleeve featured a pic of them at the San Diego Zoo just minutes before they were banned for 'mistreating the animals' or at least that was how the *LA Times* reported the incident. The back

**Above: Getting a breath of that country air . . . The Derek Taylor influence. Far right: Signed on the night The Beach Boys in Cardiff.**

cover was probably more interesting as it included pics of The Beach Boys on tour in Japan and . . . a photo of Bruce . . . he'd finally made it, albeit, on the back cover.

Three months after *Pet Sounds* hit the charts The Beatles released *Revolver* and the race was on again . . . In an attempt to keep pace with the music he was creating, Brian felt that the whole Beach Boys image needed a face lift and called in Derek Taylor (a recent UK exile who had done so much for The Beatles) to help plan a new direction.

Taylor: 'Brian took me into another room and said that The Beach Boys were a strange group; he said they had neglected many things, like artwork and pictures and press, but that now things had a shape and form and direction he could recognize and describe, he didn't want things to get away from them. He wanted everything to come together . . . We decided to have new pix taken, simple things in fields — without striped shirts — and we decided not to beat around the bush about anything any more at all . . . I lived in Hollywood then, but my British links were strong and with *Pet Sounds* out and The Beatles increasingly flattering about The Beach Boys and with *Good Vibrations* on the way, we started to pump information into England about this tremendous band, with their new plateau . . . Soon everyone was saying "genius" and the beauty of it, as with the beauty of anything, was that it was true.'

*Wouldn't It Be Nice*, coupled with *God Only Knows*, was released as a single and eventually peaked at the number eight position while in the UK the disc was flipped and *God Only Knows* rose to the number two position.

While the Beach Boys were gaining massive popularity in Europe and especially in the UK, Brian was already working on the disc that was to become a major recording triumph. When Brian was young, he remembered his grandmother telling him of vibrations — feelings that animals would receive from people and other animals, that could not be seen or heard. Invisible feelings. He used the concept to develop the feeling of good vibrations into a song. Brian: 'We wanted to do something that was R and B but had a taste of modern, avant-garde R and B to it. *Good Vibrations* was advanced rhythm and blues music. There was an era where songs would be written in twenty minutes — a half-hour . . . *Good Vibrations* took a couple of days.'

Putting the track down was a mammoth task in itself. Brian used an array of studios in his endeavour to find the right acoustics. He'd also discovered a new toy: an electronic instrument called the theremin — a little known instrument that was popular in 1940's movie soundtracks. Chuck Britz: 'The first session for *Good Vibrations* was done at Western . . . totally live . . . the whole thing. To me it was the same as when he finished in seventeen tracks — seventeen tracks later. Dennis wasn't there for the first session; Carl and Al played bass. Mike was in and out. We had a slew of musicians. Hal Blaine, Al De Laurie, Don Randy on organ. Brian usually played piano. Brian sang on everything. He had a lot of fun. The first session, everything just jelled. Again, I think he tried and tried to please everybody. Then when he was all done he went back to the first sound because it was the best of them all.'

Mike Love provided the final lyrics, but it took six months, four studios, almost a hundred hours of tape and around twenty versions until Brian finally chose the one for release.

Released in October '66, *Good Vibrations* coincided with The Beach Boys' first major tour of the UK. Kicking off on 6th November at London's Finsbury Park Astoria, their sell-out concerts took the group to Leicester, Leeds, Manchester, Cardiff and Birmingham. *Good Vibrations* became the number one hit record on both sides of the Atlantic. Back in the studio, Brian was planning a new album that he provisionally titled *Dumb Angel*, then changed to *Smile* . . . but either way it was going to be a long wait. Capitol had already begun to plunder their back catalogue, and on the very day The Beach Boys were appearing in Cardiff's Capitol Theatre, they released the first of many *Best Of The Beach Boys. Best Vol. 1* rose to number two in the UK and peaked at number eight in the US. But in fairness to their US fans, the UK compilation was a far better buy.

For their new album, Brian was at a loss for a lyricist. Asher had returned to the advertising profession exclaiming that Brian exhibited 'just awful taste' and that his choice of, say, movies and TV programmes were terrible. Asher: 'I mean, for, say, every four hours we'd spend writing songs, there'd be about 48 hours of these dopey conversations about some dumb book he'd just read — plus he was starting to get pretty weird.'

However, it wasn't long before Brian found a new songwriting partner . . . Van Dyke Parks. Brian: 'I met him at Terry Melcher's house. Listening to that guy talk, I said, "that guy's articulate, I'll bet he'll make a good lyric writer" . . . and he was. We just started working a few weeks after we met . . . We just wrote songs.'

Parks was a classical music student. He'd arrived in Los Angeles at the age of thirteen and became a child actor. He later became a songwriter mainly supplying songs for the Harpers Bizarre group (a surf band originally known as The Tiki's).

**Below: Ex-Tiki's The Harpers Bizarre who scored, thanks to Van Dyke Parks, with *Come To The Sunshine and Anything Goes*, among others.**

Parks: '*Surf's Up* was the first song we wrote for the *Smile* album.' *Surf's Up* was quickly followed by *Cabin Essence* and *Heroes And Villains*. The latter was destined to become The Beach Boys' next single. However, Capitol in England couldn't wait and released *Then I Kissed Her* from *Summer Days* as a single and it reached the top five in May '67. Mike became even more worried when he heard Van Dyke's lyrics — it must have been hard to take 'Columnated ruins dominio' from *Surf's Up* for example. Mike: 'I never objected to musical progressions . . . the only thing I ever objected to was lyrics — I think lyrics should be used to communicate. Music or sound which will communicate a feeling. Meaning and feeling together make a musical whole . . . Although I thought they were far-out, I didn't relate to them. When I heard a lyric that made no sense to me, I could appreciate it on an aesthetic level, but it didn't sit with me. I had a difference of opinion from those who did.'

Others in the group were more enthusiastic about Brian's new direction. Bruce Johnston: 'The first time I heard *Surf's Up*, I just wanted to rush out and employ an audience and bring them into the studio to applaud what I'd just heard.'

Brian found an audience for *Surf's Up* via the TV special *Inside Pop: The Rock Revolution* — hosted by Leonard Bernstein. Directed by David Oppenheim the cameras caught Brian at home, at his piano playing solo. Bernstein: 'Poetic, beautiful in its obscurity *Surf's Up* is one aspect of the new things happening in pop music today.' He also added that the song was 'too complex to get all of it the first time around'.

By the time The Beach Boys' new single was released Brian had a host of new songs in the can, including: *Bicycle Rider, Do You Like Worms, Vega-Tables, The Old Master Painter, I'm In Great Shape* and *Wind Chimes*.

However, it was while he was working on *The Elements Suite* that things started falling apart. Almost constantly high on drugs, he cut a track called *Fire*. He had the group plus session musicians dress in firemen's helmets to add to the atmosphere on the session. But the main problem seemed to be that he just couldn't complete the album, he wouldn't let it go.

As the months passed, *Smile* was still incomplete. Consistent pressure from Capitol and the group, grew daily ... Capitol planned to release *Smile* before Christmas '66 and had even produced an album sleeve. While the group was becoming increasingly unhappy with Van Dyke's lyrics, Brian began to question his own ideas. Capitol was also questioning the amount spent on expensive studio time and were concerned that Brian was becoming too far-out. Then The Beatles released *Sergeant Pepper's Lonely Hearts Club Band* — that seemed to undermine the creative originality of Brian's *Smile*.

Probably, feeling completely exhausted and disillusioned Brian dropped *Smile* but left a taste of what might have been. The first taster appeared via the single *Heroes And Villains*. Released on the newly formed Brother Label (NO:1001) and distributed by Capitol Records, the disc finally peaked at number twelve . . . a big disappointment.

A month later, the long awaited new Beach Boys album finally saw the light of day. *Smile*, with all its great promise, became *Smiley Smile* and another big dis-

**Above: Taking time out from the music industry Brian opens his health food store The Radiant Radish.**

appointment. The album's production was credited to The Beach Boys and apart from the already established *Good Vibrations/ Heroes And Villains* hits, the rest of its programme was probably their least commercial sounding set to date.

Brian began his long retreat . . . The Beach Boys were due to headline the *Monterey International Pop Festival*, but Brian pulled out! He seemed to turn his back on the whole scene.

*Smiley Smile* failed to make the US top twenty, probably due to their recent UK tour; the album just managed to squeeze into the UK top ten.

After *Smiley Smile*, the rest of the group took a more active role in their recording process and scored a number of big hits including: *Wild Honey*, *Darlin'* and *Friends*. However, they never sounded better than on their '68 nostalgic trip: *Do It Again* . . .

*Well I've been thinkin' 'bout*
*All the places we've surfed and danced*
*And all the faces we've missed,*
*So let's get back together*
*And DO IT AGAIN . . .*

Written by Brian and Mike, produced by Brian and Carl, the song became a monster hit and reached the coveted number one slot in the UK.

As the sixties gave way to the seventies, original *Smile* tracks started appearing on various albums . . . *Our Prayer* and *Cabinessence* on *20× 20* and, at last, *Surf's Up* on the album of the same name . . . adding fuel to the legend of *Smile's* greatness.

In 1969 Murry Wilson decided to cash in his last hold of his sons' affairs, and sold all his rights to The Beach Boys Sea Of Tunes publishing company to A&M.

Once the Alpert/Moss organization had acquired the company, they were unsure of what to do with their latest acquisition, and called in Tony Asher. Asher: 'Chuck Kay, who runs A&M publishing, phoned me up one day — clear out of the blue. He sounded pretty concerned and straight off he says "Listen, I'll be frank with you, Tony. I don't know if our buying up all The Beach Boys publishing off the old man was such a good idea. I mean, some of the melodies are great, sure — but take this song, *Don't Worry Baby*, for example. A great set of changes, but I just checked out the words and I suddenly discover that there's all this shit about hot-rod racing in there.

I mean, how can we get an artiste — an established artiste, someone like Wayne Newton, say — to cover a song with dumb lyrics like that? We've got a problem here, see. And, anyway, I was wondering whether you'd consider perhaps re-writing the lyrics to some of the songs all over again so they wouldn't sound so . . . dumb.'

Asher thought it over for awhile, but decided to decline such an offer. Prior to contacting Asher, Kay had very apprehensively approached Brian with the idea of changing his lyrics. Asher: 'I would have thought Brian would have gotten really upset at the very idea of his songs being altered in any way but no, he just went ahead and said "Sure" — y'know — "Do whatever you want". Chuck said it was like Brian just couldn't give a shit about it either way. He'd just given up on his music at that point altogether.'

A sad, but true epitaph to Brian and The Beach Boys sixties career. However, on a happier note, in 1974 Capitol Records released a compilation of all their 'dumb' surf and hot rod songs, it stormed the charts reaching number one and stayed a best seller for seventy-four consecutive weeks . . . its title . . . *THE ENDLESS SUMMER!*

# Surfers' Choice:
# *Listen to them whine . . .*

**The Surf Top Twenty**

1. **Surf City:** Jan and Dean
2. **Wipe Out:** The Surfaris
3. **Surfin' U.S.A.** The Beach Boys
4. **Pipeline:** The Chantays
   **Surfin' Bird:** The Trashmen
5. **California Sun:** The Rivieras
6. **Surfer Girl:** The Beach Boys
7. **Honolulu Lulu:** Jan and Dean
8. **Surfin' Safari:** The Beach Boys
9. **Ride The Wild Surf:** Jan and Dean
10. **Penetration:** The Pyramids
11. **Surfers' Stomp:** The Marketts
12. **New York's A Lonely Town:** The Tradewinds
13. **The Lonely Surfer:** Jack Nitzche
14. **Balboa Blue:** The Marketts
15. **Point Panic:** The Surfaris
16. **Let's Go Trippin':** Dick Dale and The Deltones
17. **Surf Party:** Chubby Checker
18. **Summer Means Fun:** Bruce and Terry
   **Beach Girl:** Pat Boone
19. **Baja:** The Astronauts
20. **Your Baby's Gone Surfin':** Duane Eddy

**The Hot Wheels Top Twenty**

1. **I Get Around:** The Beach Boys
2. **The Little Old Lady From Pasadena:** Jan and Dean
3. **Hey Little Cobra:** The Rip Chords
   **G.T.O.:** Ronny and The Daytonas
4. **Fun, Fun, Fun:** The Beach Boys
5. **Dead Man's Curve:** Jan and Dean
6. **Little Honda:** The Hondells
7. **Drag City:** Jan and Dean
8. **Little Deuce Coupe:** The Beach Boys
9. **Shut Down:** The Beach Boys
10. **Don't Worry Baby:** The Beach Boys
11. **Stick Shift:** The Duals
12. **Three Window Coupe:** The Rip Chords
13. **Bucket T:** Ronny & The Daytonas
14. **Little Honda:** The Beach Boys
15. **409:** The Beach Boys
16. **A.A.C.S.C.B.R.T.ASSN:** Jan and Dean
17. **Boss:** The Rumblers
18. **Custom Machine:** Bruce and Terry
19. **My Buddy Seat:** The Hondells
20. **The Scavenger:** Dick Dale

**The last Wilson/Usher collaboration finally took the flag at No. 87 in December 1964.**

**The Tradewinds scored the last surf hit with *New York's A Lonely Town*. The disc peaked at the number 32 position in February 1965.**

This book is dedicated
to the memory of
Dennis Carl Wilson 1944–1983
*And for Pat, Owen and Baldge*

The author greatly acknowledges the kind help of Liz and Gwyn Fieldhouse, Mike Grant, Richard Powell, Kay Rowley, Roger St. Pierre, Tony Wadsworth and all at Capitol Records, Debbie Bennett and A&M Records, Charles Webster, Stuart Booth and the crew at the Stills Library, The British Film Institute.
And for the use of their pictures: Capitol Records, CBS Records, Cinema International Corporation, Walt Disney Productions, United Artists, The Albert Chapman Collection, and Lawrence Sweet.
Special thanks to Peter Campbell

About the author . . .

**Rob Burt** studied graphic design and photography at Cardiff College of Art. Shortly after leaving college he became art editor on the BBC's highly successful *The Story of Pop*. He later formed his own design and editorial company. Based in Bath, his books include *Rock And Roll—The Movies* (New Orchard Editions) *The Tube—The Biggest Beat On The Box* (Purnell Books) and *Robot Galaxy* (Octopus Books), while he has also contributed surfing entries to *The Caxton Encyclopedia* and *Walt Disney's Sport Goofy Encyclopedia*.

As a companion to the book the author has compiled the album *Surf City/Drag City*. Released on Capitol Records and available from all good record shops. His other compilation albums in the genre include *The Very Best of The Beach Boys Vol I & II*, *The Surfaris: Surfer's Rule* and *Gone With The Wave* and *The Soundtrack from the movie Shutdown* (various artists).
Plus — soon to be released on MCA Records Wipe Out: The Surfaris' Singles Album.

For further enlightenment subscribe to:

The Beach Boys Stomp
22 Avondale Road,
Wealdstone, Middlesex
HA3 7RE, England

California Music
2 Kentwell Avenue
Concord 2137
Australia